Sugar in the Raw

Sugar in the Raw

VOICES OF YOUNG
BLACK GIRLS IN AMERICA

BY REBECCA CARROLL
Foreword by Ntozake Shange

THREE RIVERS PRESS
NEW YORK

Published by Three Rivers Press, New York, New York 10022.
Member of the Crown Publishing Group,
a division of Random House, Inc.

www.randomhouse.com

THREE RIVERS PRESS and the Tugboat design
are registered trademarks of Random House, Inc.

Printed in the United States of America

Design by Margaret Hinders

Library of Congress Cataloging-in-Publication Data
is available upon request.

ISBN 0-517-88497-6

10 9 8

This book is for my mom, Laurette Carroll, who raised a black girlchild in America on sheer conviction and fierce motherlove.

And to my dad, David Carroll, who introduced me to journal writing and bade me never to forsake it.

ACKNOWLEDGMENTS

I would like to thank the following foundations, institutions, schools, and remarkable individuals for their invaluable support:

The W. K. Kellogg Foundation; The W.E.B. Du Bois Institute for Afro-American Research at Harvard University; The Altamont School of Birmingham, Alabama; The Birmingham School of Fine Arts; the Urban League of Portland, Oregon; the Urban School of San Francisco, California; St. Francis of Assisi School in Brooklyn, New York; the Urban League of Springfield, Massachusetts; the Office of Equal Employment for Albuquerque, New Mexico, Public Schools; The Boys and Girls Club of Burlington, Vermont; and my editor, Eliza Scott.

John Wilson, Henry Louis Gates, Jr., Peter Glenshaw, and Sherry Lovelace, for both their individual and collective faith; Charles and Patricia Gaines, for their warmth and guidance; my older brother, Sean, and older sister, Riana, for having always been my guardian angels; Rebecca T. Emeny, for her guileless wisdom; Laura Donovan, for her continued support and brilliant sense of humor; Leah Giberson, for lifelong friendship and love; my students at NCDS, for genuinely embracing me as their teacher and then some; and Monique Cormier, still and always.

And to all of the girls who participated in this project, your voices are the future ... how lucky we are for that.

FOREWORD

As I read and read again Rebecca Carroll's *Sugar in the Raw*, I eagerly recounted sense memories of my teen years. Yet, I must honestly admit, sometimes I forced myself to relive with these young black women moments that continue to sicken me, inhibit and constrain my spirit. I think the most frequent and long-lived aspects of being colored, a woman, and alive is that our presence is still a surprise, an anomaly. Our mere presence, mind you, turns heads. What an inhospitable arena to reconnoiter, negotiate, find faith that indeed the sun does rise, if our very existence is not believable.

As both my grandmothers would say were they with us today (and I must insist that through me they are here), "the Lord wouldn't set nothing upon us that we couldn't handle." Yet this passel of young girls essentially echoes my grandmothers' axiom on their own. One by one they conjure a sense of wonder and strength, and play with not one "nevermind" if we know or care who or where they are—from Jaminica in San Francisco, whose third-grade ballet teacher attempted to squash the child's love of movement and her backside by ignoring her mercilessly, to Tiffany in Alabama, who knows to have close white friends but "not real close" ones, just as she realizes the custodians in her school are not our only role models. (But they do work hard.)

I would be less than candid to suggest that I had in any way wrestled with these issues successfully before my early twenties. Yet, Lanika, seventeen, is aeons ahead of my generation's ambivalence toward white rock 'n' rollers like the ones we saw daily on *The Dick Clark Show*:

> *"Now let me tell you a couple of things: First, having dreadlocks doesn't make you black, wearing your pants baggy doesn't make you black, talking a certain way doesn't make you black. . . . It's insulting because it reduces the black experience down to products or, at the very most, dialect."*

An openness to alternatives is apparent among these interesting and thoughtful girls as well. I remember distinctly that some professions or vocations were to be sought or refused depending on how many of the race they employed and what status they afforded the race. The race had no art historians who had mortgages that we knew of, therefore art history (even of our history) was not a good career choice. On the other hand, black people die, so doctors, undertakers, and insurance sales were good. These young women have a grounded sense of race, but their race consciousness is not restrictive in any sense. Listen to Alaza of Portland, Oregon:

> *"If I ever did go to college, it would be for cosmetology school because I want to learn how to put makeup on dead people. I would like to be the person who makes dead people look cute. I've been to a lot of funerals and*

the dead people always look so bad. They never look
like themselves; they're all gray and everything. And I'd
be thinking, You know, they coulda done their hair
different, too. *I've lost a lot of friends. And, like I said,*
I lost my brother. I think when you leave this world,
you oughta be looking cute."

At one fell swoop the myth of the sex-crazed hip-hop
girls smashes into a thousand tears of the caring sisters,
homes, and girlfriends who've already lost so much of each
other: They go to a lot of funerals. But, hey, they want to
make sure none of us thinks she's been beaten down, not
even when dreams like Aisha's of Seattle wait teeter-
tottering on droughts and class warfare in Brazil:

". . . I wanted to build my own house in Brazil on the
bank of a river. I'd want my house by a river because I
like water so much. It's so gentle and lyrical."

Recognizing in themselves a vitality and legitimacy I
know for a fact were yearned and fought for by their fore-
bears, the narrators belie hopelessness, cynicism, and gross
naïveté. Eschewing the legacy of Morrison's *The Bluest Eye*,
Latisha, Myesha, Reni, and all the others are able to cradle
our vulnerabilities as they build on strengths needed to
confront and enrich the next millennium. As Alaza says: "I
remember saying, 'Yeah, girl. It's good to be black.' And
it is."

A grown black woman, I, Ntozake, want to make witness
of the backbone, clarity, and fragile, agile spirits these young

girls and women have chosen to share with the world. Yes, they no longer obsess about shining floors, or where to sit on the bus, or why a poll tax test was failed again. Their energies are world-class, their focus global, their selves glistening in a beauty usually only mothers notice.

BEHOLD! Our Daughters!

—Ntozake Shange
2 Septiembre 1995
Filadelfia

INTRODUCTION

In the fall of my first year teaching, I had a conversation about colleges and various black girlchild issues with a student of mine, a senior. A little way into our conversation, my student looked at me with a somewhat forlorn expression and said with a sigh, "I wish you had been here when I was a freshman." As a freshman, this student had been one of the first of a handful of black students to attend the private Catholic school where I now teach. Although I had been teaching for only four months at the time, in response to my student's comment I immediately felt an eerie sense of familiarity, and of identity struggle, impasse, and melancholy.

Having been adopted into a white family, and having been the only black student and faculty member in all twelve years of my secondary schooling, as well as having been one of perhaps two black people in the eight surrounding towns that make up my regional high school, my exposure and comfort with blackness came relatively late in the game. My student's yearning echoed my own voice of years past; Pecola Breedlove's in Toni Morrison's *The Bluest Eye*; Maya Angelou's in the first of her five autobiographies *I Know Why the Caged Bird Sings*; and Ntozake Shange's in her choreopoem of claustrophobic cries *for colored girls who have considered suicide when the rainbow is enuf*. That voice comes from a place of solo identity, of begrudged and premature independence, and of crazy-making uncertainty; the price of the ticket out of that place comes by means of the soul, transferred into the current alabaster exchange rate. It is the trade-off of a lifetime, and choosing to pay the ticket offers a few options that go far beyond the now passé concept of "selling out." The first and most important option is that one is suddenly allowed the possibility of individuality and self-creation; the second is the prospect of neutrality and peace of mind; and the third, less charming and the one Pecola Breedlove opted for, is complete and utter madness. My student and I have chosen the first, and having made it through the madness, we are still struggling with the peace.

Sugar in the Raw is a nonfiction profile of young black girls in America between the ages of eleven and twenty years old. I traveled to approximately twelve different cities nationwide—a few of them twice—and interviewed over fifty girls. I made a sincere effort to include as wide a variety as possible in terms of class representation and regional location. The book in its completed form includes only fifteen of the fifty interviews that I conducted.

The medium that I have chosen as writer, at this particular juncture in my life, involves many voices other than my own, voices that are in a way channeled through mine, depending upon the subject and the material. In my first two books, it was much easier to create and develop a biographical narrative based on interviews with brilliant and established authors. It is a far greater challenge to reconstruct and recreate the voice of an eleven-year-old black girlchild from Crown Heights, Brooklyn. The reason I have chosen a genre of writing that is not exclusively my own voice is because I love words and do not presume to harbor the best ones in my mind and life alone.

This medium of biographical research and interviews also celebrates the one aspect of black culture that still belongs to black people and can neither be bought nor sold: our language. Black vernacular has been our rightful voice throughout history, and it has, in many ways, survived our souls when we have needed it the most. It is not slang, and it is not improper use of the English language; it is black vernacular, and we are the only ones who know how to speak it because ours has been a culture of the spoken word—of call and response, of gospel, of blues, of storytelling, of oral history, and of rap. Our words talk miles of love and struggle.

Obviously I have been drawn to interview and write about black people because of the natural deprivation that I felt due to my circumstances growing up. However, as I have grown older and have witnessed life in its truest, most unmerciful existence, I am surprised and assured that my individuality, my blackness, and my Rebecca-ness keep me coming back for more. I remember when I was a teenager dating young black boys for the first time, their attention more fortifying than words could possibly describe. I boldly accepted my rite of passage into this world I had silently longed for while listening with casual indifference to the voice that questioned what this naive nexus of souls might actually mean. These boys took me to task on the authenticity of my blackness; they scrutinized my language, my style of clothing, what my parents did for a living, and where I lived. The only thing about me that they readily accepted was that I was not as dark-skinned as most of the black girls who hung out at the local speakeasy in Portsmouth, New Hampshire, where my white birthmother lived (with whom I had recently reunited). That, and I could dance pretty well.

I strategically placed myself in situations where I was needed and where I needed to be, where I could become, and where I could move minds from one place to another—black or white, but preferably black. After spending the weekend immersed in black attention and livelihood, I would go back to my high school in the more rural part of New Hampshire and argue with my schizophrenia, as the captain of the soccer team and the captain of the field hockey team gleefully paired up. I was perpetually without a date, a good friend to many, a girlfriend to none.

Regardless of my family and school environment, growing up I always knew that I was black. I was particularly reminded of this when my best friend of ten years was forbidden to take me to the junior prom because I was black, warned that if we did go together, no pictures would be taken. At that time, I didn't think so much of other black girls per se, but of black people, wherever they may have been. I clung to a contrived notion of specialness as a result of my governing factors; being compassionate toward other black people did not seem relevant, but thinking constantly about where I could find them did. I couldn't even muster up affection for my black female peers back at the speakeasy, who looked at me with salty and invidious expressions. Only now, as an adult, have I been able to revisit my own black girlchild experience with kindness and to wonder ingenuously about the experiences of other black girlchildren.

My mom sometimes shares a funny story with my friends when I go off on one of my "blacker than thou" tangents. When I was six years old, my mom searched high and low to find a dance teacher for me. Ironically, she found a black dance teacher. After my first class, I came home full of excitement and energy, going on and on about my professional dancing aspirations. When I paused briefly, my mom said to me, "And isn't it great that your teacher is black?" And I replied, "Oh yeah, she is, isn't she?" That is the truth. It had not occurred to me.

I feel now that in my work as an author, a biographical researcher, and an instructor of history and literature, I can no longer afford such blissful insouciance. What I can afford to do is to look at what I have before me and to assess it in an evolutionary, intelligent, and passionate way so that it is accessible. This is not a pledge of *multiculturalism* or *diversity*, words that belong in the socially constructed lexicon of race relations euphemisms, but a pledge of human existence in the present, with kind and courageous acceptance of the past.

I was raised in a family of creativity and will; it was not "racial." I have a black student at the school where I teach who, when things are not going her way, takes heart in saying, "It's racial." I allow her that freedom because it's funny. Just like when the folks gather together in our name and play the dozens, or call each other Negroes or Negresses, or tell each other to "stop actin' your color!" But I also

17

know, like the air I breathe, what is "racial" and what is not. I have had no choice but to learn the difference because I have existed in the margins of both white American culture and black American culture. I have been forced to find ways in which I can navigate myself *out of* the margins but not necessarily *into* the mainstream.

My research for *Sugar* was both remarkable and insightful. In Brooklyn, where I lived for a year, I visited a small Catholic school, which was predominantly black with a spattering of Hispanic students. I spoke to the eighth-grade girls about writing, about my project: how it was for and about them, and perhaps they would like to help in its creation. At first they just looked at me. If I recall correctly, I was wearing jeans and a T-shirt, maybe a suit jacket over it—not terribly bohemian, more minimalist. I wore my hair naturally in a close crop cut, as I do now. One girl raised her hand and asked, "How come you dress so . . . so . . . different? And why you wear your hair all natural—don't you have trouble with the naps? Where are you from? Excuse me, but what kinda black lady are you?" I smiled, looked at her, and said, "The kinda black lady that you wanna know."

I went on to tell these girls that the "kinda black lady" I was, was the kind that wanted each of these girls to feel self-aware, strong enough to self-invent, and creative enough to make her life look any way that she wanted it to look. I told them that I was the "kinda black lady" who has seen the inner workings of both black and white America, and that it's *real* serious. I told them that I was the "kinda black lady" who writes books, and who celebrates and honors her cultural heritage. And I told them that I was the "kinda black lady" who preferred to be called a black *woman,* but that *Rebecca* would do even better. The girls were very different after that, and the atmosphere in the classroom where we were talking changed dramatically. "So you mean," said another girl, "you're not tryin' to be like other black ladies? You just tryin' to be you?" Exactly. It's not the only way, but it's one way. I was amazed at some of the expressions and responses I would get from these girls when I told them that their lives were their own, shielded by their very own implements of war.

From Burlington, Vermont, to Birmingham, Alabama, to Roxbury, Massachusetts, to Seattle, Washington, to Atlanta, Georgia, young black girls in America are often not heard, or rather, their lives are dictated for them by society, resulting in unnecessary feelings of entrapment. In some cases, many black girls don't know that individual accountability is not a myth or a crime: It is what makes it possible for us to live together on the planet as human beings.

My life's work has been to build a bridge between notebooks and street signs, to cultivate an urgent relevance between the two. We spend lots of time engaged in discourse about the human condition: We write notes, articles, books, and other forms of extremely well-written analysis, particularly on the subject of race relations. Yet, when we go outside, we can't understand that red means "stop" or that DON'T WALK means "don't walk": red as in the color of a stop sign, as in the color that flows from our bodies when we are wounded; DON'T WALK as in there are cars coming, as in don't go there. It is a matter of truly learning how to unify instinct with intellect, to civilize our instincts and to revere our intellects. *Sugar in the Raw* is a tribute to the virtue of street signs and first-person testimony.

—Rebecca Carroll
December 1995
Cambridge, Massachusetts

"I breathe hurt every day, but I'm still here."

—STEPHANIE
Fifteen
Roslindale, Massachusetts

*"Why should I have to sit here and watch
America imitate a culture they don't understand? Shoot, I
ain't got time for all that mess."*

—ELIZABETH
Sixteen
Mattapan, Massachusetts

Sugar in the Raw

LANIKA

Seventeen
Birmingham, Alabama

I went to an all-black kindergarten, with all-black teachers, and my neighborhood was all-black too. The first time I had contact with white people was in the first grade. It wasn't really a big deal because me and my friends just sort of stayed to ourselves. When I was in grade school, we lived in an area where the black people were middle class and upper middle class—doctors and lawyers—and the white people were poor white trash. So it was kind of extreme in terms of perceptions about race. But the result of that extreme was that in school, the blacks stayed together and the whites stayed together. And nobody really forced us to integrate. None of the black teachers—or *any* of the teachers—taught us about race or gender bias; they just accepted the segregation as the natural order of things. They believed that people self-segregate, and if the black kids sat at one table in the cafeteria and the white kids sat at another, it was no big deal. Then when I entered high school, things got real different.

The whole concept of my school is that students come here because we are different—talented or gifted and serious about specializing in our education. So the teachers are always trying to undo that tendency to self-segregate and telling us that there needs to be unity among us. When I came here it was the first time I had ever heard anybody tell me that the reason I should integrate is *because* I am different. Before it was always, "You're different, so if you feel more comfortable around the people who are different in the same ways that you are, fine." I have come to welcome integrating with other types of people and have learned so much just from talking to someone who I probably would not have talked to before. It only makes sense to meet and learn from other people who aren't like yourself. If you only spend time with people who are like you, how can you ever learn anything?

I'll admit that it was kind of jarring to come here directly from a really segregated situation. At first I was unsure about this being the place for me. There are two hundred kids at this school, and it runs from seventh to twelfth grade, so you get to know just about everybody really fast.

When I first got here, I noticed right away that the black twelfth graders were cool with the white twelfth graders, so I knew that something kinda different was going on here. Then I was intrigued and thought, *Let me see what I can do here.* And it has been very interesting. You know, sometimes I can't believe what I hear and find out. For example, there's this girl I know who is in the drama department, she's white, and for her class assignment she had to write a monologue. I got to hear it today, and she was saying, ". . . It was my first date, and I was eleven years old . . ." and right out loud in front of everybody, I was like, "What!" I couldn't believe she was talking about dating at eleven years old. It seems that for black people across the board the dating age is sixteen. I don't know why, maybe because it's also the driving age, which is the first sign of real responsibility. But white people be dating and wearing makeup at like eleven or twelve. To them, it's no big deal, but to me it's very strange. The important thing about these sorts of differences, though, is that we be aware of them. The girl reciting the monologue said to me afterward, "Whenever I perform this monologue again, I'll always think of you blaring out 'What!' " You know, we could laugh about it.

I have two younger sisters and I haven't really pushed for them to come here, but I would like to see them go somewhere that is at least similar to this school. The fact that they are still in a segregated public school system is very upsetting to me. The middle school they both attend has actually become mostly black, even all the teachers. So they are not really exposed to any other races or cultures, which I think is a fault on the part of the public school system.

Segregation is a terrible mentality to cultivate; it turns quickly into ignorance. My sisters don't understand that in order to progress in society, they need to be exposed to all kinds of people, and that alienating themselves because of their race will only bring pain. The way their school is set up, there is a black counselor for the black kids and a white counselor for the white kids—they all don't even have to see each other if they don't want to. The school has about 3,500 students, maybe 100 of which are white. I ask my sisters if they ever talk to any of the white kids and they're like, "Uh-uh, no." The principal is black and the assistant principal is white, and the two of them don't even really interact. I just feel like my sisters are missing out, and that they are going to come away from their high school experience unprepared to deal with the greater society at large.

I realize that there are some Afrocentric beliefs out there that would have black people just interacting with black people: going to black colleges, working for black businesses, and never concerning themselves with white people. And I can understand and appreciate these beliefs, but what it all boils down to in our society is that white people are in charge. They own the majority of this country. So it is sort of ridiculous and unrealistic for any black person to think that he or she doesn't need to deal with white people at all. I'm not advocating being all up in white people's faces, but I think that we can learn a lot from white people, not simply because they are white, but because they are different, with their own set of individual values and ideas. See, I like to get into people's minds to see how they work. I like to find out what makes people tick. It helps me to learn more about myself.

What I do have a problem with is people trying to be something they're not. At my sisters' school, there are white people who try to "act" black. Now let me tell you a couple of things: First, having dreadlocks doesn't make you black, wearing your pants baggy doesn't make you black, talking a certain way doesn't make you black. Shoot, I've seen white kids putting grease in their hair just because that's what black kids do! It's insulting because it reduces the black experience down to products or, at the very most, dialect.

I work at a music store after school and on the weekends. I have this one male coworker who is white, and he goes to the same school that my sisters go to. The atmosphere in the store is real laid back, and me and my coworkers can talk to each other and joke around. One time when we were just about to close the store, I had a line of people at my register and so did this white coworker of mine. While we're working the register, he started talking to me about this white guy who had come into the store the other day and was acting black. He said to me, "Yeah, you know, this guy listened to black music, he talked black, and when I leaned in to give him his CD, he even *smelled* black!" Well, I'll tell you, all the people in both of our lines just sort of stared at him, and I was really offended and embarrassed. It was too late to drop it at that point, so I asked him, "What exactly do you mean he *smelled* black?" And he was like, "You know, that smell; black people have a certain smell." So me and a couple of my black coworkers—in front of the customers—just had to go off on him! He told us we were taking it the wrong way and I wondered what other way there was to take it. I was like, "Why don't you tell me about this smell? Maybe because I'm black, I can't smell it, so maybe you better describe it for me. Because shoot, I'd like to know about that smell." He got real apologetic after that.

The next day at work, he and I had a little conference with the manager. I told the guy that I wasn't trying to hold anything against him, because I don't like for there to be friction or static in a working environment but he was out of line. His defense was that he had black friends in school with whom he was always cracking these sorts of jokes and they never took offense. Clearly he was making an attempt to prove that he wasn't racist, yet the way he went out of his way to tell me about his black friends and what they were like told me that he might not be racist but he sure is prejudiced. I tried to explain to him that he may well have black friends who are comfortable with him and the things he says, but that as a white person, his making a comment about black people having a certain smell in front of customers and coworkers was both inappropriate and stupid. He had only been working at the store for about a month, and maybe he didn't know better. But if he had given it some thought, he probably wouldn't have said it to begin with. Language goes a long way; you have to be careful with it, especially when you're talking about race.

As far as the racial atmosphere in my home goes, there is a strong sense of blackness. We have lots of paintings by and of black people, we have lots of books by black authors, and my parents are very proud of our black ancestry. For the past few years, I have collected newspaper clippings about various racial issues that I think are important to know about and learn from. My aunt lives in Connecticut, and she sends me plays and articles that offer different views and are relevant to the black experience in America. So I try to maintain a strong sense of what it is to be black in society.

I definitely value the differences from culture to culture and race to race, but I can't see dating a white guy. My boyfriend now, he goes to public high school. He's black. There are only six black guys at my school. I don't really know why I wouldn't think about dating a white guy. I guess for me personally, because I try to read and find out about my history as much as I can, it's pretty hard for me to get beyond the image of white slave masters raping their black women slaves. It's an image that really sticks out in my mind and has obviously had a scarring affect on me, especially since the flip side of that history has bred such anger and resentment in black men. I am always seeing black men with white women, and I can sometimes tell that they just think they're aaallllll that because they got what white men got. It's disgusting really, but history runs thick in all of us. I mean, black men used to get lynched just for looking at white women, and I suppose now they feel like they're free not only to look, but also to *have* white women. So they're going to.

I do have some real problems with interracial relationships, but I don't judge people who want to go that route. It's hard to imagine having to explain to a biracial child his or her history without serious conflict. I have a biracial friend who I think is fine with it, but that's because she lives with her mother, who is black, and my friend has leaned more toward black culture than white culture. I consider that there must be a lot of internal struggle for biracial kids because if you have brown skin, you might as well be black.

I study ballet at school. The reason I started dancing is because when I was little, I didn't have any rhythm, and my dad told me that I needed to get some coordination going. So I started taking all kinds of dance lessons: ballet, African, jazz. I was falling all over the place at first, and people started to think that there might be something wrong with me. I slowly started getting better, and my ballet teacher at the time noticed that I had a natural turnout, which is first position in ballet when your toes point out in opposite directions but your heels are touching. So I decided to stay with ballet. And I love it. I've been doing it for thirteen or fourteen years now, and over the years I have realized that it actually relieves a lot of stress.

What doesn't relieve stress, though, is the fact that classical ballet is an historically European dance. It is quite evident that the positions and movements were not meant for black people. There was a black girl here a while back who wanted to study ballet, but she had a swayback, which is a back that dips in real far. The teachers told her that it was too dangerous for her to study ballet. See, anybody can have a swayback and not be bothered about it, but if you have a swayback and are studying ballet, which requires you to push your hips up and under, it can be potentially damaging to your spinal cord. This girl's parents ended up threatening to sue the school for racial discrimination. The whole thing got completely blown out of proportion and the girl never came back.

I admit that it can be difficult as a black student of ballet. See, although African dance has changed over the centuries, one component of African dance that has always been the same is free movement. African tribal dances were all very contracted and released—a lot of bending down, jerking, and flowing motions—while European dance has always been very stiff and straight postured. That's why I take an African dance class twice a week, because when I first started to study ballet seriously and was doing it like three and four hours a day, my knees started giving me trouble. African dance allows my body to work out its kinks.

I'm going to tell you, though, even the tights for ballet are not meant for black people. The tights are pink—the color is actually called European pink and is meant to blend in naturally with the white girls' skin. But when I put those pink tights on, you can see my brown skin coming through. Most of the time I wear a black leotard and black tights. I told my ballet teacher that I wasn't even tryin' to wear pink tights because they are not made for me to wear. How am I gonna put those tights on and pretend that my skin doesn't show through? Ballet shoes, too, both slippers and point— European pink. Traditionally ballerinas are supposed to wear their hair in a bun. Well, it's not healthy for me to wear my hair in a bun because sweat accumulates on my scalp, which causes breakage. The white girls wash their hair everyday anyway, so it doesn't matter for them.

And then there's the hip issue. Ballerinas are also supposed to be real petite, you know, with real small waists that curve in real slightly and then curve back out only the littlest bit more. But your hips are not supposed to stick out, and mine do. Sometimes my teacher will tell me to put my hip down, and I have to tell her that that is where it is, and it's not going anywhere, never mind down! There are about ten black girls studying ballet here, ten out of forty. The ten of us support each other because we enjoy classical ballet and because we are disciplined and good at it. I dance ballet and support other black girls who do because I am famous for doing things that people tell me I'm not supposed to. Besides, nobody can tell me that Louis the Fourteenth discovered dance. Africans were dancing long before he came along. All those Europeans were over here in America with the plague and all the Africans were over in Africa chillin'! We had it together over there and I've researched this, so when people try to tell me that Africans were all tribal barbarians back in that day, I have to tell them a thing or two.

The single most distinctive thing to me about being black and female is knowing that I am part of a culture that has come very far, a culture that has struggled to maintain its integrity, spirit, charisma, and intelligence. With that knowledge, I carry with me the certainty that I can be and do whoever and whatever I want.

JO-LAINE

Fourteen
Brooklyn, New York

There's this girl I know at school who described me once in reference to herself: she said, "Well, I'm light-skinned, but Jo-Laine is *black*." What is that? Even though she's black, too, because my skin is darker I can't be described as anything but black, while she can try to be some thing else? I said to this girl, "Yes, your complexion is lighter, but we are *all* black." Being light-skinned or having real nice hair that doesn't kink up or whatever is definitely something some girls like to boast about. I don't even think

35

they know that it might hurt my feelings or even bother me at all. I don't think they think about anything but having the opportunity to be something other than what most people think being black is.

Those same girls who boast about being light-skinned feel that they are prettier than me, like they have an advantage over me. But I really truly feel that it doesn't matter what your complexion is. I don't let simple things like that get to me, but I do think about it. I mean, black is just a color. What matters is what's inside, or rather, how you feel about yourself inside. Because you can have a lot of good inside you, but if you don't feel good about it, then it is lost. You can have the best hair, the best eyes, the prettiest complexion, but none of it's gonna get you anywhere if you don't feel something inside.

My mother and my little brother are lighter than me, and I remember when I was like seven or eight asking my mother why I was so much darker. She said, "Don't worry about it, Joey. Don't base who you are on your complexion." And I haven't. I really do believe that my personality and my intelligence is what's going to get me where I need to go. Besides, I don't even call myself black, I call myself *mahogany*. I think it's so foolish the way *Essence* and *Ebony* talk about different makeup foundations for black women, you know, they'll be having these silly names for every shade, but the emphasis is always on making your skin look lighter so that you can get that "café-au-lait complexion" or whatever. It has nothing to do with anything. It's bad enough that we only have two magazines to look at, but when these two magazines start turning over to the way society wants to see us, then we're in trouble.

Being a part of black culture feels very good to me. I heard or read Maya Angelou say once, "I am the hopes and dreams of the slaves." I love that, and that's how I feel, too. I feel so proud, and even though I know that no matter what I do or say, there will always be somebody who's going to try and put me down or make me feel like less of a person than they are, all I have to do is think about how far we've come. It was worse for my parents and my parents' parents, but if they could do it, then I know I can go out in the world, hold my head up high, and make even more changes for my own children one day.

My mother and father have always talked to me about the different kinds of people there are in the world and all the different ways in which they will try to con me. For example, I may apply to a college or for a job one day, and have an interview with a white person who may say to me, "You're very smart and qualified, but you're not what we're looking for." What is that? If I'm smart and can do the job, then I should get it and they're not being honest. But I can't say that, because it's a losing battle, a long legacy of people who can get away with situations like that. I have to take it in stride and be able to come up every time I'm put down.

Some people in my neighborhood have preconceived notions about Brooklyn girls. They see some black girls out in the street misbehaving and misrepresenting, wearing real tight, short skirts or whatever, and people automatically think that all the black girls in Brooklyn are like that. Sometimes I struggle with this image of being black that I don't really want to stand behind or be lumped in with. Like on television, oh my goodness, there is this one cartoon on Saturdays about kids, and there's a white girl with her hair in two neat little bouncy ponytails or in pretty barrettes, and then a white boy with either nicely cut or shaggy hair, but the black boy always has a high-top fade and the black girl always has her hair in two big bubble-looking balls. The white girl is always the cautious one, while the black girl is always snapping her fingers, having attitude and all that.

A personality is something all its own; it doesn't have to do with race. I have attitude sometimes, but not because I am black. I get attitude when a situation calls for it. The reason why television shows like that cartoon use those kinds of stereotypes is because there actually are a lot of young black kids who uphold those images, but also because it's mostly white people making the shows, and that's the only image they know or feel comfortable with. All I'm saying is that I don't want to be seen as just any one thing simply because my skin is black. Unfortunately, you know, if you like hip-hop and wear hip-hop clothes even if you just stepped out of Harvard, you're going to be stereotyped. That's why people need to speak for their own selves and tell people who they are, otherwise we'll never truly be known.

I was on my way to choir rehearsal the other day, and I was wearing a short skirt—not too short, but short—and this older black woman said to me, "Don't you feel ashamed to be wearing your skirt that short?" And I was like, "No, uh-uh." I said to her, "What *do* you mean?" She told me that I looked like a tramp or whatever, and I just walked away. Afterward, though, I thought to myself, *Look, it doesn't matter how I dress or what I wear, people are going to judge me no matter what.* I try to just focus on being a good person. I'm not thinking about that woman and her judgments because I know who I am. If that woman had judged me on my personality, then I would have taken issue with her, but she went on and judged me on something as simple as my skirt. Like I said, "No, uh-uh."

There are certain situations when we have to prejudge people in terms of being safe and aware of what can happen, based on what we know can and will happen. Like if I'm walking down the street at ten o'clock at night and five men are headed toward me, black or white, I'm going to have to make a prejudgment: Should I stay on this side of the street or cross over and walk on the other side to be safe? I'm probably going to cross the street, because those five men could be the nicest men in the world, but I know what I've read and seen on the news, and I know what can happen. If they are in fact nice men, they won't be offended that I was protecting myself. And if they aren't nice men, good thing I crossed the street. Of course, I probably shouldn't have been in the street at ten o'clock at night in the first place.

I really do try to treat people the way I want to be treated, and I want to be treated as a human being and judged on who I am. If somebody doesn't take the time to know me and keeps judging me because of the way I look, it becomes hurtful and I feel incomplete. But if someone says something because they don't know better and then change their mind after getting to know me, then I feel complete. Whether that person likes what they see in me or not, at least they are seeing the whole person and I can defend myself from my base as a whole person.

Some of my friends are rowdy, and on the weekends or in the summer, you know, we walk around outside, ride the subway, or whatever. I've been in situations where me and my friends will be standing on the platform waiting for the train and some of my friends start acting up. I notice that some white people get scared and move to the other side of the platform because they don't know what my friends are going to do. They don't even know us. And it'll be like broad daylight! I can see prejudging people if there is real danger involved, but not when you're scared of what a bunch of thirteen-year-olds *might* do. That's when the line is crossed between cautionary prejudice and racial prejudice.

I recently got my report card: 99 average in science, 91 average in math. I had been in the honors program for a long time, but they didn't put me in the honors program this trimester because of my attitude. Now, the reason for this, I think, is because some of my teachers have a real hard time admitting they could be wrong and they don't want to be questioned. I think the whole purpose of a good education should be about making a place for kids to ask questions and look at things real closely. Some teachers at my school disagree. I am very strong-minded. If you try to tell me that I didn't go to A and I did go to A, I'm gonna let you know. I don't scream or whatever and I never presume that everybody's going to feel the same way I do, but I'm gonna let you know. My mother taught me that. She has always taught me to speak up for myself and to make my point calmly and clearly.

My math teacher and I have a long history of not getting along. One day I just came into class, put my books down, and listened and answered. I know I don't need to antagonize my teacher, but as my mother said, "You make her work for her money." I decided to just listen as well as I could, be attentive, and then ask smart questions. And that is how I moved my average up from an 87 to a 91. I will never compromise my strong mind, but I am willing to learn how to use it properly.

I go to a Catholic school, which prides itself on discipline. We have to wear uniforms, and our parents pay tuition for us to learn. I don't have a problem with discipline, but I do have a problem with a misunderstood definition of discipline. I had a teacher tell my class once when we were talking and acting up, "I could just sit here and watch you and I'll still get paid." I will never forget that. When I told my mother about it, she said, "Well, then, you just sit and watch her back, because you're *not* getting paid!"

My mother and I are very close. We are closer now than we've ever been because I'm old enough to see that she has been there for me and believes in being a parent. She truly wants me to be a well-rounded person. One time I was arguing with her about starting this confirmation class on Saturdays. I didn't want to do it because all the other kids were outside playing and I wanted to play, too. My mother put her hands on her hips and said, "Look, I'm your mother *and* your father, and you're going!" Even though we all live together, when my mother is disciplining me, she speaks as both parents and my father does the same. So it's never like, "Go ask your father" or "Go ask your mother." No, 'cause I'm looking at both of them either way. And you know what? I love my confirmation class. It's actually fun.

What I mostly like about confirmation class is the choir practice. At first, I thought all of the girls in the class were going to be snobs. But they all turned out to be really nice and we have a good time together. And I do take the religious part of it seriously. God is a Supreme Being. Sometimes I get God and Jesus mixed up and I can't figure out who I'm supposed to pray to. But my mother told me that God and Jesus are one and it doesn't matter which name I want to address Him as. And God does work in mysterious ways. One time my mother read my diary and I got in trouble for what was in it. I prayed so hard to God, I was like, "Please, please God, if you don't let Mommy beat me I promise I won't ever lie, and I'll be good"—you know, all that. I got in trouble, but my mother didn't beat me. I had written about kissing a boy and also some bad things about my mother after we had gotten into some fight. I promised my mother that I was going to make her proud, and after that whole thing, I ended up getting into the honors program at school.

I realize that organized religion is an institution that some people think can be limiting, you know, or controlling, but I don't feel limited or controlled. I'm so young too, and what I know of religion and the God I pray to is only positive and helpful. I think it's a good support system for me because sometimes when I act up or whatever, I always reflect on my actions and apologize if I am wrong or do right by someone if I haven't dealt with them right. I think all of that has to do with God somehow. I mean, I'm the one who's making amends, but there is this force in me that makes me come straight and I think that's God.

I have one brother who is five and two sisters, twenty and ten. My little brother is the apple of my mother's eye. I used to be the apple because my older sister is from a previous relationship my father had with another woman, so I was my mother's first daughter. I was so spoiled. My baby boots are plaqued, my birth certificate is framed, and there are poster-sized baby pictures of me at my grandparents' house. Then my sister was born and she's fine. She gets whatever she wants from my father. And then my brother was born, and he was the first and now the only boy. I remember when he was born, he was so white-looking at first that me and my little sister were like, "Mommy, are you sure that's your baby?" And she told us that he sure enough was, but that when we got home we'd have to get some shoe polish and paint him black like the rest of us. He's darker now but still pretty light.

The kind of girl I am has everything to do with the kind of woman I think I'll be. I know that I am bold and straight-forward. When it comes time to deal with boys and what-not, I will make clear who I am and how I expect to be treated. Right now, I really don't need to be thinking about any of that—you know, condoms and diseases and getting pregnant. I'm not thinking about any of that, not yet any-way. A lot of girls be thinking they're grown, having sex and everything, but they only get hurt and used in the end. It's just pitiful, really. I'm talking about little kids here. To me, twelve, thirteen, and fourteen are still little kids. As far as I'm concerned, it's too much of a hassle. Sex can wait.

When it comes to black history, I like to think about Mary McLeod Bethune, because in all of the books I have read and in school, slavery is talked about like, black people couldn't do this, couldn't do that. But Mary McLeod Bethune went out and built a schoolhouse out of cardboard. Nobody was going to tell her that she couldn't do for herself and for her people. That's inspiring and truthful. That's the kind of truth I take with me out into the world.

White kids don't really have to sit down and think about their role models or their history. They don't need to because this whole society is their role model, and their history just keeps repeating itself. Black kids have to search for positive black role models and we have to teach ourselves about our history. Trouble with the way things were and are when it comes to the history of black and white America is I like things to go my way. I don't give into what anybody else is trying to tell me to do. I choose people to admire who are like that, too. If some kids asked me to go to Flatbush to look at some boys or whatever, and they say, "Come on, come on, Jo-Laine, it's gonna be fun," I say, "Look, it's going to be fun for *you*. I don't think it's going to be fun for me, so I'm not going." I'm going somewhere else and it isn't the same place everybody else is going.

LATISHA

Fourteen
Portland, Oregon

I had stopped going to school for a month or so when I realized that I was starting to forget what I had learned during the time that I was in school. My cousin was in a program at the Urban League and she got me an application. I've only been in the program for two or three months. It's okay so far. The teachers are good, but some of 'em have attitude. When people are rude, just ignore you or say foul things or whatever, that's attitude. Guess it comes from their backgrounds. A lot of people say I got attitude, but I don't really see it. The only reason people be saying I have attitude is because I stand my own ground. Like when dudes try to push up on me—ask me if I got a boyfriend or whatever—I tell 'em to mind they own business 'cause I'm not givin' them no play. Then they say I'm stuck up with attitude. But I feel like I'm a happy person, you know, try to be smilin' all the time and whatnot.

Most of the time, reason I don't wanna talk to none of these dudes is cause they be gang-affiliated. Most of 'em just wanna get some anyway. It's not that I've had bad experiences with guys, you know, the boyfriends I've had are always friends first. That's real important, to be friends first. But all my homegirls have nothin' but bad things to say about their men. A friend of mine just got pregnant and her boyfriend asked if it was his. She told him yeah, and he denied it and told her that all he wanted from her in the first place was just to have sex with her, he wasn't talkin' about no baby. See, all these niggas want these days is sex, and if we keep giving it to them, they gonna think they can get it anytime they want it. It's disrespectful.

I think the difference between me and my homegirls who give it up so easy is that I'm aware of all them diseases and troubles having sex can bring on if you're not careful. Some of these girls out doin' what they doin' know about the diseases too, but they get attitude in full effect, and be sayin' how they can do whatever they want with their body. Strange thing is, I think lettin' dudes have sex with them makes them feel good about themselves in a way. If they have sex, then the dude is gonna keep being nice so he can get some more. It's only when something bad happens that

dudes be showing their true colors. There are some gentle-
mens out there who will treat a girl nice and maybe stay
with her, but you can't barely ever find 'em. Most dudes are
all in gangs, or already dedicated to a female, or just plain
messed up.

You can tell a dude is in a gang by what he's wearing.
They usually wear Dickie pants, with a blue or a red belt
hanging down from the pocket. They refer to the colors as
"flue" for blue, which is the color for the Crips. And "ded"
for red, which is the color for the Bloods. You gotta be
careful, too, because if you're wearing one of those colors,
you can get in real trouble. Even if you are not gang-
affiliated and you are wearing either red or blue, you can be
identified as gang-affiliated even if you don't want to be.
Gang members be speakin' differently, too. They speak English and all, but they cover it up with their own kinda
gang-style talk. Sometimes they speak in pig latin. It's pretty
easy to know who's in a gang, and when you see somebody
from a gang, you need to keep walkin'.

Don't do nobody no good to be in a gang. I mean, it's
pretty simple: If you wear blue, you gonna get shot. If you
wear red, you gonna get shot. Even gang members' families
are classified as being part of that particular gang, so the
whole family is put in jeopardy. I have one brother who's a
Blood and one brother who's a Crip. The Bloods and the
Crips are against each other, but if it really came down, I
think my brothers would have each other's back. I know if a
Crip was shootin' on my brother who's with the Bloods, my
brother who's with the Crips wouldn't agree with killing his
brother. Sometimes I'm walking down the street and a car

full of gang members will drive by, hollerin' about how I'm just like my brother and whatnot—you know, depending upon which gang it is in the car. I tell 'em I'm not in gangs, but they tell me not to come at them with all that 'cause if my brothers are in gangs, then I'm in gangs. Both gangs.

I have one brother who's not in a gang and he's in the same urban education program with me. Then I also got a younger sister. My moms tries to get my older brothers out of the gangs, but they are nineteen and twenty, so they think they grown and can do whatever they please. Moms is always telling them to stay inside the house, but they go out anyway, and then sure enough somebody gets shot. Until my moms sees my brothers walk through the door, she's sure it's one of them who's been shot, always reason to worry. Whenever there is anything on the news about the gangs around here, my moms gets all hyped and hysterical until she finds out that my brothers are all right. It worries me only a little bit because I know that gang members look out for their own and also because my cousins and other relatives are in gangs around here too, so my brothers'll be all right.

I've never heard anything about my brothers being involved in any kinda gang rapes or whatever. But I can't be sure. They're both fly and the females be sweatin' them constantly, always wanna get with 'em. My older brother's girlfriend just had a baby, but he don't help take care of it 'cause he always out gangin'. I feel bad for that baby, 'cause she gonna grow up wondering where her dad is all the time or worrying about him getting killed. My brother says he loves his girlfriend, but I think the only reason he stays with her is cause of her baby check—you know, the money she gets from welfare. She always be givin' him money and he don't never pay it back. So he's stealing his baby's money. His girlfriend is in love with him, at least she say she is, but I don't think lettin' yourself get used or usin' someone else is what love is about. My brother doesn't even think the baby is his 'cause he says his girlfriend fooled around with other men when she got pregnant. But the baby looks just like him.

My father lives in California. I met him and I don't like him. When I was younger, he beat on my moms all the time. He beat her with a hammer and a gun and left her for dead. Us kids had to see all that, see her bleeding and rushed to the hospital. It hurt so much to see her like that. Now we just consider our father dead, 'cause we don't got no love or respect for him. I think that's why my brothers are in gangs 'cause they need older male role models. Gang leaders be in gangs for a long time. My oldest brother told me the reason he be in and out of jail so much is 'cause he didn't have no guidance from a father figure. My moms is much better off now. She's going through a lot right now, and sometimes we don't see her for a while 'cause she's been in and out of jail, too. First time was for accessory to a burglary. She got three years for that. Then one time she was at the scene of a crime and there were no witnesses to testify that she didn't do anything. She's been in the wrong place at the wrong time a lot. But now she's tryin' to clean her life up and we know she loves us.

My brother who's in this program with me is my role model. He's real smart. And also my aunt, who I stay with sometimes, is also a role model for me. She is a Christian and has a good job. She's always telling me I can be somebody and I do want to be somebody. I want to get a good job and have a family when I'm ready. Her daughter, my cousin, is thirteen and she already got two babies. Yeah, she was pregnant with the first one when she was eleven, had it when she was twelve. I don't want that. It's not a choice I'm gonna make anytime soon. Everyday I try and listen to what I know I got inside of me, you know, my personal strength, so I don't become a victim of society.

There are a whole lot of things I want to do. I want to be an accountant because accountants make lots of money. I want to be a comic because making people laugh seems like a good profession and it feels good when people smile after I say something. I want to be an artist because I like to create other worlds. I know I have a long road ahead of me, but I don't feel disadvantaged because I know well enough to listen to myself and to folks around me who are honestly trying to help me out. If I put my mind to it, I can do anything. When I wake up in the morning, I don't think about being black or about being a girl, I think about just making it through the day.

Sometimes, you know, I wonder what it would be like to be somebody else, somebody with lighter skin, longer, straighter hair, and pretty blue eyes. There don't seem to be no real famous dark, dark-skinned women with nappy hair out there. I know I'm pretty and all, but I also know I'd be prettier with lighter skin. That's what everybody says anyway. Besides, it would be so nice to be able to walk down the street and not have to worry about getting stopped by the

police, just once not to worry 'bout some Caucasian police-
man holdin' a gun to my head, askin' me 'bout which gang
I'm in. Crazy.

I'm not scared of dying because I know the Lord will
take care of me. I don't wanna die or nothin', but I know if
I get killed it is because my time has come. If I could tell
young black girls in America anything, I'd tell them to be
hopeful and to know that there are always options. They can
always turn to God. Even if we can't hug or touch God, He's
there for all of us. I would also tell them to take responsibility for their lives and to seek out people who will be
supportive. And you gotta start out by finding yourself and
knowing that you can give support back, so that it's even
and not about charity or nothin' like that. The most important thing, though, is to try and stay grounded, even when
the world is spinnin' around you.

NICOLE

Seventeen
Burlington, Vermont

We lived in a few rural places in Pennsylvania for a while after I was born, and then we moved to Pittsburgh for a while, and then we moved to Burlington. What I remember the most about living in those different places was that the first grade school I went to was very, very white, and I was thought of as the "white" black girl. I was very skinny and pretty, and shy. Then when we moved to Pittsburgh when I was eleven or twelve, I attended a predominantly black school, which was a defining experience for me.

It was time for a change. I saw that black boys liked black girls—black girls who were shapely, who had big hips and butts. So I ate. And ate. And ate. Finally I got my own big hips and butt. I got myself a black boyfriend and dove headfirst into what I thought, at that time, my being black was about.

I hate Burlington. There isn't enough diversity. There's a lot for Vermont, but there's not enough for me. My mother is white and my father is black. I don't consider myself biracial, or black, or white. I consider myself Nicole, although when we visit my white grandparents' house and there are other family members around like my cousin, it is he who is seen as the "good" child. He is pure white. I am the black sheep of the family, just like my mother is the black sheep of her family for dating my father. In society, I am made to feel like a black sheep for precisely that reason of my white mother and my black father getting together and having me, which was considered wrong at the time and still is in some people's minds. I am the walking representative of that wrongness.

We all have the ability and the resources to be individuals, but when I walk down the street I am clearly identified as a black person and am discriminated against accordingly. I don't blame my parents and I don't blame people for their ignorance. Nobody has done anything wrong here, but it's like having to work at a job I didn't apply for. I alone have to come up with the added strength to deal with racism, and that isn't something I bargained for when I came into this world. I don't draw from the loving union my parents had when they got together to make me; I draw from the love I have for and within myself. Basically, I'm the one who is going to be here in the end. I'm the one who is going to have to defend myself. I can tell my mother when I am discriminated against or whatever, but I'm the one who has to look it square in the face.

I think when people act stupid they are holding themselves back and ultimately losing out. I'm the one winning in a situation where someone is acting stupid toward me. I have the advantage because when we throe down, in the final analysis I'm the one with the knowledge and the sense of self. The racist is the one who will forever have in his or her mind that I am bad and that they are good, which is a lie. It's just not true. Period. End of story. I get so tired of people believing in their heart of hearts that they can win or achieve anything by making someone feel inferior. I think that's how I have developed my defense mechanisms against racism; I just got so tired of hearing the rude remarks and having teachers and counselors tell me that there wasn't anything I could do about it. Because there most certainly is.

When I was younger, my teachers would tell me not to beat up these kids who were saying racist things to me because then they would win twice: I would look like twice the animal they were telling me I was. What made me mad was that I didn't think they were winning at all, never mind once or twice, and I felt compelled to do them the favor of making that completely clear. My teachers would tell me just to walk away, that I would come off more powerful if I just walked away, which, in retrospect, I suppose was true, but it took me a long time to truly believe that. It's all well and good in theory, but it doesn't exactly eliminate the feeling of having a knife twisted around in your gut. Now, as I've grown older, I find that it is really important to just be focused and to stay as positive as I can. I do still get angry, though. I have a real temper. Emotions and theory don't really go hand in hand, so it can be very difficult for me sometimes. But I have learned from my mistakes.

On the consensus checkoff lists that offer little boxes next to black, white, or other, I refuse to check just one box. I check them all off because I am all of those things. My mother told me that when I was born and she was filling out my birth certificate, the nurse asked her to write in *mulatto*, which my mother did not do. I think the word is incredibly negative and degrading. It sounds like a sickness. The part of me that is black-identified doesn't fit into a category or a box. Society has such awful ideas about black people, and I don't want society to decide for me what it means to be black. When I think of being black, I think of kings and queens and history and beauty and authenticity.

You can call me black if you want to, you can call me mulatto, you can call me biracial, you can call me whatever you please, but I'll still be Nicole. Are you going to remember me as "that black girl"? No, you're going to remember me as Nicole if you've taken the time to learn my name. And those who haven't taken the time, I don't care to be remembered by. It's Nicole today, it'll be Nicole tomorrow, and it'll be Nicole when I die. I don't care if you have something against black people, or if you have a problem with interracial relationships, or if you don't like biracial kids. I don't care. But if you are talking to me, call me by my name.

I realize that my geography allows me to be less concerned and less political than some about race. I know that my race issues here in rural Vermont are different from those for a black girl in Queens or Detroit or wherever. I know that in other circumstances I might be asked to choose between races and side with one or the other. I am not unaware of these facts, and I fully anticipate having to deal with them head-on when I leave Vermont. I plan to travel when I turn eighteen, to explore other cities and ways of living. And if I am ever asked to choose between black and white, to in some way please one race by denying the other, I will more actively and aggressively try to make world changes.

My mom told me this story about when me and my younger sister were toddlers: It was summertime, and my mom was pushing us in a double stroller. She was walking near a whole busload of Canadian tourists. One woman looked at us in the stroller, and then looked at my mom and said, "It must be terribly difficult to give up these Fresh Air kids at the end of the summer." And my mom looked at this woman and said, "Lady, vaginal deliveries. Both of them." Obviously there is a lot of work to do in terms of educating people or maybe just in finding ways to ignore the ignorance. We've already spent decades trying to make it clear that we are all human beings on the same planet with the same hopes and dreams, for the most part anyway, but nobody seems to be listening.

I go to the only public high school in Burlington. It's predominantly Vietnamese and white, with a handful of black people. It's very different from my school in Pittsburgh. I just can't seem to really understand this whole idea of being "black" in one particular way or in the "stereotypical" way, which is an important thing to think about for those black people who *are* black in the "stereotypical" way. These folks need to know that they can be more than just a stereotype. My mother's current boyfriend is black. She has had several black boyfriends and one black husband, and she doesn't eat chitlins, she doesn't drool over fried chicken and watermelon, and neither do we. Neither does her boyfriend and neither do my black friends at school. There are black people, and of course white people, too, who give up who they really are to fit a certain image. I can't see myself doing that.

I see a lot of young black men around here with white girls, which is really frustrating. It doesn't even figure into my feelings about my mom having consistently been in relationships with black men. I don't know where the frustration comes from; it just feels bad to see a young black man with a white girl. I ask these brothers why they're always going out with white girls and they tell me it's because black girls have attitude problems, which immediately makes me want to scream. *All* black women have attitude problems? *All* of us?! And do they really think that the attitude comes from being black? Can't black girls be self-contained just like white girls without being labeled as having an attitude problem? And it wouldn't bother me so much if I felt there were something legitimate going on here. But it is easy to see what these young interracial hook-ups are about and I think it's a shame.

My boyfriend is biracial, but he only identifies himself as

black. I think being male and biracial makes you more susceptible to peer pressure and stereotypes than being female and biracial does. It's much more confusing for my boyfriend because there is really only one acceptable image of black men in this society, so if you are identified as black, biracial or not, you'd better assume that image. Even though I think my boyfriend is strong enough to be his own person, I think the pressure to be a certain way is almost unavoidable for him. He lives with his white mother, and lately he's been carrying around *The Autobiography of Malcolm X*.

The only thing I can do is to try and create goals for myself. It doesn't really matter where I come from or who I come from; it matters who I am and what I can be. Reaching the goals that I make for myself will be a challenge and a struggle, sure, but what is life without struggle? For black people, life without struggle is no life. And what will happen if I sit there and wonder what I could do with my life? Nothing. Nothing will happen. And nothingness is not worth it. There are no limits to what I can do with my life. I strive for so many things all at once. My goals and my focus might change from day to day, but at least I know that I have the choice to make goals and to direct my own life.

I watch the news a lot and I have seen reports on how schools devoted to black students—both secondary schools and colleges—are slowly being eliminated because predominantly white schools are now saying that black schools represent segregation. This is very upsetting to me because I really want to go to a black college. I feel like I *need* to go to a black college. And then of course, the predominantly white college students get upset when black students are recruited

and given scholarship money. How will we ever learn anything if we don't hand over the baton? Where is the strength
in keeping things stagnant?

I am eager to experience as much as I can. I want to go
to Africa. I want to see all of the United States. I want to go
down South because I have heard about the blatant and
violent racism that has occurred and continues to occur
there and I really don't believe it. I need to witness it for
myself before I believe in it as truth. I want to see the black
man driving through a white neighborhood and getting
stopped by the police just for being black and in that neighborhood. Racism in Vermont is nothing compared to what
I see on the news, in the movies, or on television. And I
know that the formula comes from some sort of reality, but
I need to see that extreme ignorance acted out. I don't think
that my life is so provincial that I am exempt from any sort
of racially horrifying circumstance. My strength and my
struggle are open. I am not afraid to open them wider.

ALICIA

Thirteen
Springfield, Massachusetts

The projects I live in are not a negative place to live like a lot of people might think. I feel safe there and everything. I mean, I know that a bullet don't have no name on it, but I trust the people in my neighborhood. I know almost everybody by face at least. There are a few white families but mostly black and Puerto Rican, except the Puerto Rican and white kids are always trying to be black. They wish they had the same opportunities that we have. You know, they wear baggy clothes and listen to rap music and everything, but for example, when we have a talent show at school, it's mostly the black kids who perform. I don't know why, we just do because we can. I think some white and Puerto Rican kids wish they had that same kind of natural talent and ability, you know, the opportunity to have that kind of talent and ability, too. I'm not sayin' they ain't got no talent, I'm just sayin' that black people have been dancing and singing since we were in Africa and it just sorta comes to us, is all.

There's nothing in particular about Springfield that I like. It's real segregated. I like my friends and so it don't matter where I live. My friends are mostly black, but some of them are white. Like I said, they want to be black. They want to talk like us and everything, and try and have black personalities or whatever, but you know, if they got white skin, they're not black. I think whites or Puerto Ricans or any other race can act as black as they want to, but they can't be what we are. It's not something that can be acted. I'm not sayin' it's all about skin color either. It's just that being black is about our ability to express ourselves and the way we express ourselves and then our history in America.

Sometimes I think about black people from way back. My history teacher in my summer upward bound program told us that the first person on earth was a black woman. I'm not sure he know that, but he was sayin' that if a black woman has a baby with a white man, the baby is still black. And if a black woman has a baby with another race, the baby is still black instead of mixed. I half believe that and half don't. Because I do think that kids are mixed if they have one white parent and one black parent 'cause they have both black and white blood up in them, but at the same time, I know that if they look black, they gonna be black.

My family is black. I have a stepbrother, but he don't live with us. My mother and father work for Springfield Action Commission. They do a lot of work to improve our community. I go to school at Rebecca M. Johnson School, which is right around the corner from the projects I live in. It was founded in 1992 and it's a public school for mostly black kids, but that's because it's in a black neighborhood. There's a lot of schools in Springfield, but I've been at this school since it opened and I like it a lot. It's not special or anything, but it's like a school especially for my community. I've been to a few different schools, but I don't think about them much.

I remember my baby-sitter who was like a godmother to me. She was Muslim. She taught me everything. She taught me how to go to the bathroom, how to tie my shoes, and how to look at books and start pronouncing words and everything. She was somebody who I could look up at and see myself. I knew how I looked by spending time with her, you know, it was okay for me to look and feel like a black girl. I didn't have to be scared of what that meant. She got cancer and passed away when I was in the third grade. I miss her and I still go visit her husband. I don't know where her grave is. I think it's better not to know so I can keep her in my heart.

Since having her in my life, sometimes it's hard to tell whether I'm being given a good education and everything. Because sometimes teachers don't really take the time they need to or sometimes they teach the same things twice without knowing it. The way I try to tell if I'm getting a good education or not is if I can hear in my mind how my baby-sitter might have taught me, and even then, if I can hear her teaching me, I'm still not always sure if what I'm learning is valuable. I guess if I'm in class and the teacher asks a question, and I know the answer, then what I've learned is valuable.

I never feel disadvantaged like with money or anything. My parents both work really hard and we don't live without. Sometimes I find that I want more than I have, but usually my parents will find a way to get for me what I want and need because I'm the only child living in the house. If they can't get whatever it is, well, then, I'm just one of the ones who don't have. My mother is like a friend to me. She's really nice and smart, and she loves me like a mother should. You know, both my parents are strict with me, but they always give me the benefit of the doubt and we can always talk things through.

I understand why my parents might be strict because I see what some other girls do, you know, getting pregnant or whatever. I know that I would never put myself in that situation, so it's like double security knowing that my parents are trying to not let me get into that situation. I base my future on going to school, getting through it, getting through college, and after I reach those goals, then I'll worry about having kids. It's not like most black girls can't figure this out on their own and it don't really set me apart from them that I already did, but I don't know why they don't, and I don't know why everyone always be looking at black girls getting pregnant and going on welfare, because it's not just black girls. Everybody makes bad choices and everybody falls into bad situations. The thing that is sad about it is when people don't use their natural abilities to reach a goal in life and to be somebody.

When we were slaves, white people made us feel like we weren't never gonna be nobody 'cause we were just sittin' around gettin' beat on. We didn't have jobs. But now, you look around and you see how far we've come and how far we can go. There's an eighteen-year-old black girl in my community who's running for mayor. She's done a lot of work with the youth in our community and for the Urban League. A lotta people say she's not gonna make mayor, but I think just the fact that she's trying and knows that she can try is really good. If she makes it, I know she's gonna try and make a lot of positive changes for our community. There was a seventeen-year-old black boy shot by a white police cop a while back. The cop shot the boy because there had been a report of a stolen car, and the cop thought the boy he saw was the one who stole the car. But he was wrong and the boy was killed. It was mistaken identity. The boy was black and so he died. So this girl who's running for mayor was the one who organized all the marches and protests against the cop because he only got suspended for a few weeks. She did all that she could to bring justice. She wasn't gonna sit around and let something like that just happen. I look up to her and have mad respect for her.

Seeing what that girl has done and can do makes me want to make some changes too. I know I can help my community now just by being a good person, but I'd also like to help get rid of gang violence. I know people who are in gangs, but none of them are my friends. I don't see much violence myself. There have been shootings in my community, but I've never seen it happen. Very so often there will be murders and stuff, but not like every day or whatever. I don't worry too much about getting shot. I get involved in summer programs to keep me off the streets.

If I didn't have things to do with myself in the summers, I'd be out there hangin' out with my friends and whatnot. I don't get into much trouble usually, but I do get angry and I've been in some fights. Very so often somebody makes me mad, and I try to deal with it by talking first, but they don't listen and I get heated and gotta release my anger somehow. I've gotta be pretty angry to hit somebody, but if someone disrespects me for no reason at all, I think that's grounds enough to hit 'em. If somebody calls me names or whatever, first I'll just keep to my business and go on. But if it keep goin' on, keep goin' on, then I'm gonna get mad. I know something really bad could happen, because this is the nineties and everybody be packin', and very so often people get shot and killed over nothin' at all. I'm trying to stay away from that type of situation because I know if I get mad, it's on.

Hitting somebody is just like a reflex, you know. I didn't learn it and I'm not tryin' to hurt anybody. It's just the pressure of being angry needs to be released. I think it's better to talk things out, but it don't work. What works is hittin' somebody. You know what I mean? Like I know the best thing is to be mature and talk and all that, but most kids don't be listening to anything or nobody. I don't need to prove I'm strong or nothin' like that, I just need to take care of what I'm feeling, is all. I could probably find another way to release my anger, but for now I just try and avoid situations where I'm gonna get angry in the first place.

My best girlfriend helps me out a lot. She's real funny and makes me laugh. She's usually in the same summer programs with me. I've known her since I was like two years old. We live on the same street in the same projects, and anything I need to tell her, I can tell her. She's like a sister to me. She's real funny and she don't even know it. But she be doin' like funny dances or whatever, or make a joke out of something I say that sounds real serious. I trust her a lot, and she makes me feel like my problems aren't really even problems. She just kind of puts them in a way that is real but not at all bad.

I have friends who are boys, but no boyfriends yet. I'm just not ready. I like boys as much as girls because if we can all laugh and whatnot, it's all good. I have a friend who's a boy and I call him "my boy," you know, 'cause he makes me laugh, too. I know that if we have an argument or whatever, we can sit down and talk about it and all that. He's a friend and I know we gonna go through stuff 'cause that's what friends do. Boys at this age are kids just like girls. Later on it gets more confusing and I'll deal with it when the time comes.

I take one day at a time, you know, just like that girl running for mayor; I don't sit back and just let things happen in my life. I know in life you can't be a follower, you gotta be a leader. And I think being a true leader is about being true to yourself. What I like most about myself is that I am me. I know that I'm me because there's nobody else to be.

RENI

Fourteen
Birmingham, Alabama

I think the concept of this book is very inspirational because it is so important for black girls to hear what other black girls are thinking. People create who they are based on their experiences with and their exposure to other people. I just read a book by Maya Angelou called *Wouldn't Take Nothin' for My Journey Now*, which was wonderful for me because it sort of showed me the world and how big it can be if you are aware of what is going on in other people's lives. So in terms of this project, even if I wasn't in it, I would say that it is very necessary because it makes it possible for black girls to see ourselves in the world, saying and doing all kinds of different things.

As far as my own perceptions of being black and female go, I've only just recently begun to think about it because the age I am now is when all those sorts of things start to matter. Before this past year, I didn't think much at all about my image as a black girl in America. But one particular incident that happened recently increased my awareness and aroused my curiosity about race. There is a small suburb close to Birmingham where there is a fairly well-known public school. At this school there is a high-school sorority that is very popular and traditional. First of all, you will never see a whole black family living in this suburb. I can go there and feel safe, and I've never experienced blatant racism, but if you are black you just know that you are not welcome there. Some of my friends at school live in this suburb and have talked about rushing for the school's sorority. These particular friends of mine are white. There is an unspoken rule that black girls are not allowed to rush this sorority. It is not so much that I would ever want to rush the sorority because the school and its environment are very rich, white, and snobby. And sororities are not particularly appealing to me anyway, but it bothers me that it isn't even an option for me to think about. I think the reason my friends are attracted to the idea is because of the tradition behind it. Some of the girls' mothers were in the sorority and they feel they need to carry on the tradition. In my opinion, it just turns into a popularity contest.

I have more white friends than I do black friends, mainly

because there aren't that many black kids at my school and it would be almost impossible not to make friends with the white kids. But also because I am African, which doesn't exactly allow me to fit in with a lot of the images and ideas American black kids' have about being black. My one close black friend at school is also African, so we share that in common, but all the rest of my friends are white. I have good relationships with them and I like them a lot. I feel like my friends are my friends before they are anything else, and if a conflict comes up between us that involves culture or race, I believe that we can at least try to understand each other. The conflict could be something as simple as the difference between black hair and white hair, although some white girls actually *like* my hair. Or it could be something as complex as my native Nigerian culture and some of my cultural behavior, which can be difficult to understand if you don't know that much about Nigeria.

I've been going to the same school since fifth grade and I'll be going into tenth grade next year. My mom taught me to read when I was very young, so when I got to preschool I already knew most of the things they were trying to do. I started kindergarten earlier than I was supposed to, so that's why I'm fourteen and going into the tenth grade. When I first arrived at the school I'm at now, I did feel different. But the school really tries to base its curriculum on the diversity of the student body and the individual minds that are a natural result of that. After a while, I just sort of forgot that I was different, or rather, was able to enjoy my difference.

I would never say that prejudice doesn't occur at my school or in this society, or that I've never been stereotyped.

But it is less of a blow for me than it is for some people, I think, because I understand people for who they are and what they see. For example, I have a friend at school who is extremely spoiled and hasn't been exposed to many other cultures or races other than her own. The only black person she had seen before coming to school last year was her maid. When she started school, she was somehow immediately drawn to me. The reason she provided me with was that she liked people who listened to hip-hop music and could dance well. She was new to the school, so I was pleasant to her, although she was terribly annoying. She can still be intolerable, but I began to realize that she doesn't know any better. She isn't necessarily trying to hurt me when she makes prejudiced remarks; she is only seeing what she is able to see. My friends and I have accepted her for who she is even if we have to break it down for her sometimes. She does have the ability to be very sweet and kind at times.

I think the superior attitude of that particular friend is mostly a problem of her own because she doesn't realize that she is not growing when she makes thoughtless comments and that she is only enhancing her own very obvious insecurity issues by putting other people down. Just the other day, she and my friends and I went to an outdoor music festival where we got a lot of attention from boys, mostly white. All of a sudden she said to me, "You need to go find yourself a homeboy!" She was intimidated by the fact that a white boy might find me, a black girl, attractive. She's the type of person who will bring someone who she thinks is less attractive than her to a party, especially if it's someone who she thinks is heavier than she is. And the thing is, she is very pretty, in a sort of cherubic way, and she's very solid and well built. She just has some learning to do and sometimes we have to preach to her, but she'll get through it. I consider it an interesting learning experience to have her as a friend. I don't patronize her; I just accept her for who she is.

I've never really given that much thought to the way I look. Of course at this age everyone is talking about how important it is to be pretty and thin, but I've always thought, *How can you not like someone because they don't look good?* I find that once I start to like someone, they automatically become beautiful to me. It is completely dependent on the person. There are a lot of conventionally beautiful people out there who have extremely repellent behavior.

I don't feel necessarily judged by other black kids at my school for having white friends, but then I don't really pay attention. It's not a big deal to me. Until the fifth grade I went to an all-black private school, and I still see the kids from that school during a three-day camp seminar I attend every year. My experience at that school was fine, but again, because I am African sometimes people were very prejudiced about what that might mean. Some of the kids thought I was from the jungle and never wore clothes. Because we were so young at the time, part of their misconceptions came out of immaturity, although you can also find adults who think that Africa is uncivilized.

For me, being African means honoring my parents and having a deep respect for my native culture. I don't think I would consider myself exclusively African, but I also wouldn't consider myself African-American. There are certain things that African-Americans have experienced and continue to believe in that I do not. I do not share with them the history of slavery. I think about it, but it's not my history. There are also certain things that I think are expected of you if you are to be considered as "truly" African-American: listening to rap music, being able to dance and perform and keep up with all the latest hip-hop moves, being angry and resentful at white people. When I attend the camp seminar with the kids from my old school, it is not immediately comfortable. I can't just kick back. I can get to a certain level with them, but there is still something in the back of my mind that keeps me somewhat reserved. I know that when I left that school and moved on, some of the kids there judged me for leaving my "African-American" identity behind. But at the school I'm at now, I've been able to become more of who I am, more of an individual. They always welcome me at camp, but sometimes little things will come up that I'm out of touch about, like new dance steps. I can't keep up with all the latest hip-hop dance steps because nobody dances hip-hop at my school. So sometimes I feel sort of left out and I know that I can't really be in their clique, but it doesn't actually matter to me.

I was in the mall the other day with my mom and my sister, and this black guy who was hanging out with a group of his friends kept on saying, "Hey!" He said it like a few times. I didn't think he was talking to me because first of all, I didn't think he would behave that way when he could clearly see that I was with my mother. But I guess he was talking to me because when I didn't turn around or respond to him, he said, "Oh, I see, she's been hanging out with those white folks too much!" So in his opinion, because he could not get my attention in the middle of the mall by hollering, "Hey!" I had been spending too much time with white people. It's too bad that for so many black people in America being black means feeling vengeful toward white people.

When slave history is brought up in school or in conversation, it scares me because I think a lot of people think that American society is heading back to slavery. At the camp seminar, we have lecturers come and speak to us. One time, this man who was delivering a lecture to us kept referring to "The Books," like the fact that black people are going to be enslaved again is in "The Books." I had no idea what "books" he was talking about. Then he told us this story about chickens and eagles. He used the story as an analogy for the situation between whites and blacks in America today: The chickens represented white people and the eagles represented black people. As the story went, a young eagle had somehow been placed in a society of chickens, and he had lived his life being laughed at and ridiculed. You know, he would try to use his talons to peck like the chickens, but it didn't work. So one day, this eagle was in a field by himself, feeling sad about not fitting in, when he saw a bird fly over him with incredible grace, power, and beauty. It was an eagle, but of course he didn't know he was an eagle too. The eagle in the sky came down and said to the orphan eagle, "What are you doing with these chickens? Why do you let them ridicule you? Don't you know that you are an eagle and that you are better than these chickens? Your talons are not used for pecking, you could kill these chickens with your talons if you wanted to!" So the old eagle taught the young eagle to be strong and powerful, and they both lived happily ever after with other eagles. I don't know if anybody else interpreted that story in the same way that I did and I didn't say anything about it, but I felt like it was kind of weird to use a story about putting other people down to convey a moral message.

There is this common mentality among some black people that we are never to forget slave history and that black people are entitled to feel vengeful if they so desire. Of course, slave history will never be forgotten, but it shouldn't automatically give blacks the freedom to do whatever they please, nor should it for whites. We are supposed to learn from history, not dwell on it or let it fester inside of us. In order to reconcile with slave history, we have to reach a point of awareness, and the sole purpose of the reached point is so that we can then move on. I don't think I've quite reached that point for myself, but I am also not afraid of what I will have to go through to get there.

When I look at the history of black people in America, I feel hope. And hope is needed. I am willing to bring mine to America.

SAVANNAH

Fourteen
Philadelphia, Pennsylvania

I was raised to understand that I am black and female, and that those who are white and male are not to be trusted because white men are dangerous. It was weird sometimes too, because my mother would occasionally date white men when I was younger, and I had been told to stay away from white men, or at least those wielding bats.

I didn't really understand problems I had growing up until now. I didn't have a brother or a sister to say, "What's that about?" And I didn't know that the things I was experiencing or going through were actually not at all normal. When I was much younger, my mother was a fierce cocaine and barbiturate addict. We would make dinner together when I got home from school and then she would go to sleep. She wouldn't wake up until the next time we made dinner. I thought it was just normal that mommies slept all the time and that housekeepers took care of kids. I didn't actually witness my mother doing drugs until I was seven. We were in Manhattan on the Lower East Side visiting a friend of hers. I remember it very clearly because I was watching television at this man's house, and you know that drug commercial with the egg—"this is your brain, this is your brain on drugs"—well, that was on television. My mother was holding this cream-colored business card and she folded it in half at a forty-five-degree angle. There was cocaine in it. I didn't know it was cocaine at the time, but then I saw her pour this white powder up her nose using the folded business card. Then I made the connection. I was like, "Oh, my God, my mom's on drugs!" My mom told me that she wasn't doing drugs and that what she was putting up her nose was a natural herb called Golden Seal. I got very upset and wanted to leave, but the man whose house we were at and who had given my mother the cocaine wouldn't let us go. We ended up staying for a long time.

My mother stopped doing cocaine a couple of years ago, although she still gets high. She's been off alcohol for thirty-seven days. I used to worry about her, but I don't anymore because I can't. It'll kill me if I worry as much as it takes. We talk about it but don't really get clear on it. I don't do drugs or drink at all. I don't need the added complexity in my life. There are severe genetic addictions on both sides of my family, crazy-ass addictions, all sorts of addictions. So me and drugs and alcohol do not coexist.

I'm going into the tenth grade next fall. I'll be going to a new school in New York because my mother will be working and touring too much next year and won't be able to take care of me. I had the choice of either going to boarding school or living with my aunt in New York. I will not go to boarding school. I'm not a good person if I'm away from home and not home as in one place; if I'm not in my house, then I am with a member of my family—not to mention the fact that I don't want to be sent away to a school with two thousand white people. That's just not my cup of tea. The school I just came from was wonderful. I entered in the fifth grade and just left this year at the end of my ninth. It's a great private school for girls, a good, liberal, independent school. From prekindergarten to eighth grade, it's just girls. In ninth and tenth grade, the art, music, and literature courses are coed. The boys who come to the school in the ninth grade but only for certain courses keep going to their own boys' school across the street until the eleventh and twelfth grade when my girls' school becomes totally coed. So the schooling starts out building a girl's own voice and then teaches her how to use it when it's integrated with a boy's voice, which I think is a great approach.

A lot of people ask me what it's like to have a famous mother. And even more people tell me how lucky I am to have such an incredible mother. But it is hard. I think her work is brilliant. I think that *she* is brilliant. She has a talent for capturing things in words and images that people might think could not be captured. She works not just with the words she uses but with the spaces and the spelling and the color as well. I write some, but I don't write like she does, and that's not what I'm going to do for a living. I'm going to do theater. I'm going to act. Film gets on my nerves, but I understand that if I'm going to be looking for the real money, then I'm going to have to do some film. Acting on camera is just very tedious to me. I've done commercials and we do a lot of on-camera acting in my acting class, but you have to be so subtle. The medium requires that everything be toned down. I like more freedom to express myself. Certainly I get some of my creativity from my mother and also from my father, who is a painter, who I haven't seen since I was seven, but I don't think my creativity really comes from anywhere. It just is.

My parents got divorced when I was nine months old. After that, they shared the parenting and I would spend equal time with both of them. Then my father moved to New York. My mother and I were living in Houston and I would fly to New York by myself to visit him. After our last visit in New York when I was seven, he just stopped talking to me. Our last visit was fun, though. We did what we would always do when I visited: We'd go to Little Italy to eat and then just hang out. He has never sent my mother child support money, and after we stopped speaking for no apparent reason, that started to make me angry. One Christmas about two years after our last visit, he sent me this black cameo necklace on a strand of real pearls with a typewritten note that said: "Merry Christmas, I love you. Dad." I was completely unhinged by it. He didn't even sign it. He didn't call, he didn't do anything but send me this expensive-ass present. I couldn't call or write—write where? There was no return address. There was nothing.

Now I don't really make anything of it all. I don't wear the necklace. I can't. I wore it once, but I felt like I was choking. I would have rather he gave me nothing or hadn't made any contact at all. The whole experience was bizarre and upsetting because love doesn't have symbols. Love doesn't manifest itself in objects. Love has members, people. A cameo on a string of pearls is not a symbol of love, it is a symbol of financial security. Whenever I'm in New York now, I keep expecting to turn around and see him standing there. I don't think there's anything I'd like to say to him. And I'm certainly not interested in seeking him out. I don't particularly care to have him in my life at all.

Some of my mother's boyfriends have served as positive male role models, but my grandfather has been the constant in my life. I like men okay; they can be cool. I think it's funny how all these white feminists sit around talking about how men and women are equal and all that good shit. But see, I don't think men and women are equal. I think that two piles of clothing are equal. I think men and women are two pieces of a puzzle and that we need each other. Men have things that women need and women have things that men need. It's not that I have no use for feminism, it's that I don't like the way a lot of women use the word. To me, feminism is more important not so much in this country, but in places where women are being mutilated, cut up, and used as chattel. In this country, feminism is more of a free-falling power struggle.

In places like India, Afghanistan, Asia, Africa—places that Americans don't really look at for any other reason beyond tourism—women are being broken down and disrespected on a far deeper level than women are here. In this country, women may not be allowed to use our abilities, but our abilities are at least recognized as worthy of preventing. We may not be allowed to have the jobs at which we would be the most productive and we may not be allowed to make the same amount of money, but we are allowed to work. We have the option of busting our asses to try and get the more productive jobs and the bigger paychecks. It's not that I think American women shouldn't complain or get loud and protest, it's just that I don't choose that particular struggle for myself in light of a more profound struggle that exists outside of my personal reality.

I choose to deal with being black first. For me, being black is not something I know or understand or grasp or realize, it's just something that I am. Being black is about everything that I do, everything I feel, and everything I say. There may be words I can use that go around the feeling as sort of an outline, but I can't translate it into English as we know it. The outline is about being one with "the first": I am connected to my mother, to my grandmother, to my great-grandmother, and so on. That connection is the sort of connection that a white person could not possibly understand. There are distinct senses of pride, pain, struggle, and fight in my blood. These senses came from my mother, which she got from her mother. There is this burden that takes the form of a crown we all wear to remember that a woman or a man to whom we are related had to go through the Middle Passage. I wear that crown every day.

That's why I don't understand black women being with white men. Black women have watched their men get beaten and flogged and were there for them afterward. A woman who is related to me experienced that, which is something that turns into a connection I have with every black man who walks and lives today in this country. White people are not bad as a whole. There are good white people who are not innately malevolent. They have their own connections with one another just like black people do except their historical connection doesn't carry the same sort of integrity. Black people and white people can laugh and have fun and intellectualize, but it doesn't go much deeper than that. It can't.

I think I'll end up living in Philadelphia when I get older. I am an urban child. The country just really seems dangerous to me. I mean, if something happened, you know how long it takes for the ambulance to come? Kids have to ride bikes and shit to get to places. There's no bus, no subway. It scares me. I need access to everything all the time. The reason I wouldn't choose New York to live is because everyone has this tainted tunnel vision and nobody makes eye contact. In Philadelphia, people make eye contact. It's about making that fearless contact with another human being.

I'm a very instinctive person, but I'm not superstitious. Instinct comes from within; superstition is based on hearing something from somebody else, from your grandparents, friends—you know, folklore or whatnot. I rely on my gut for all the choices and decisions I make, from people I make contact with to crossing the street at a certain time of the day. And I am never wrong. I have always valued myself before looking to someone else to value me. It's a difficult and continuous process, but no matter how much I've been broken down, I've tried to find the place within myself that is willing to keep going. This struggle is survived by my passion—I mean passion in general. I don't do luke-warm. . . . If I feel something, I feel it in its entirety.

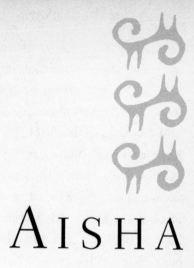

AISHA

Thirteen
Seattle, Washington

I live in a very quiet neighborhood in Seattle that is made up of both black and white families. It is what I have known for my entire life. I go to a diverse public school with all different types of races. Beyond the typical followed-around-in-the-store story, I don't give that much thought to being black. I have as many black friends as I do white and I think all of my friendships are based on honesty. The black community in Seattle is spread across the city, although there are very poor areas of the city where mostly black people live. I've been to these areas and their schools are run-down, unsafe, and not very well kept. I have a friend who goes to school in one of these areas. She goes to her school and I go to mine. It doesn't define who we are.

I know that I am black, but I don't think I'm different. My family and home carry in it a strong sense of black culture. We celebrate Kwanzaa, we talk about black history, there is always black literature and art around, and we *are* all black in my family. My mother is a writer and I have read her first book, which is a children's book. But I haven't read her novel, which came out last year. I went to kindergarten through second grade at a school called The Garvey School, as in Marcus Garvey. I learned a lot about black history and whatnot. The school was all black, and we talked about everything and read about things that have happened in history that might help us to understand things that are happening today.

In the third grade, I went from an all-black school to a mixed, predominantly white school. That was a transition just in terms of looking around and seeing white faces. At first I felt uncomfortable instinctively, and then there were things that just seemed wrong. For example, one of the counselors told me that my scores were not high enough to be in the honors program, but they were. My parents told me that those counselors were trying to hold me back and that I just needed to persevere. I ended up getting into the honors program.

I know that more things like that will happen to me as I get older. But I think my best quality is that I am smart. I want to be a brain surgeon and a concert violinist. I can't be stopped from playing the violin, and being a brain surgeon just requires intelligence, discipline, and dedication. I've got that. My parents help me a lot and encourage me to think. My father is an ultrasound technician, so I have learned a lot from his precision. I love history and I'm all right in math. Whatever I focus on, I just love to get into it and explore all sorts of ways of looking at it.

My relationship with my parents is good. Sometimes we argue, but then, I argue with a lot of people I guess because I like to engage with people, especially if there is adversity involved. It's not about convincing people to see things my way; it's about learning another perspective, which ultimately makes both of us smarter. I talk with my friends about the work we do at school and what we think is useful, as well as the things we think are not useful. I look for smart people to be friends with, people who are funny and weird, like me. I'm not interested in being intimidated; I'm interested in being myself. So I look for people who are smart and who don't try to make me feel bad about being smart too.

I realize that most girls at my age think about the way they look and boys and whatnot. I feel that I accept the way I look. My parents have asked me if I want to straighten my hair or get a perm, and I don't because there is nothing really wrong with my hair the way it is. When I was younger, I had this one really close black girlfriend. We have grown apart over the recent years because she has chosen an entirely different path than I have. She has lots of boyfriends, she straightens her hair, and although she is very pretty and smart, she is not very interested in school. She manipulates her parents and gets whatever she wants. My parents have encouraged me not to go the same route that my old friend has chosen, but I probably wouldn't have chosen it anyway. I have completely different priorities than she has. My strong suit is what I can do with my mind and my personality. Yes, I am beautiful too, but it's not a priority to me.

This year in my language arts class, my teacher gave us an assignment to split up in groups and choose a skit to perform. The group I was in chose an idea that included a slave part. One of the boys in the group said, "Okay, Aisha, you be the slave, and I'll be the master." And I looked at him dead-on and said, "Why don't *you* be the slave and *I'll* be the master?" We ended up not doing that particular skit but another one instead. The point is, I can go through my life every day and feel determined and ambitious, not feel limited and all, but whether or not I dwell on it or choose to make a big deal of it, racism happens all the time. I think it's important for this to be known, but it's not going to prevent me from doing what I want to do.

I've been playing the violin since I was in the fourth grade. My friend played it; at that time I was playing the clarinet. But I liked the violin better, so I asked my friend if she would teach me. When I began to get a grasp on it, I asked my music teacher if I could play the violin instead of the clarinet and she said fine. I love the concentration, the sound, and the mood of the violin. Most people don't know that you can play a lot of different kinds of music on the violin. You can even play hip-hop. I think what I like about the mood of the violin is that it is sort of melancholy, which lets me think about the things that are on my mind or deeply inside of me. It also lets me feel like I am part of the instrument.

As far as world politics and problems are concerned, I worry deeply about homelessness and hunger. There was a time when countries would help each other out, but now that global economies have gotten so bad, especially ours, we either can't afford to help or we don't want to help because we want to keep it all for ourselves. We have made some bad choices in this country centered around the value of money versus the value of human beings. I don't think there is an immediate resolve. I think we are here on a trial-and-error basis and we'll probably end up wiping ourselves out, making way for another species to evolve.

I sort of believe in God, but I don't believe that He created the heavens and all that. I believe in evolution. But I also believe that when there is a bad enough problem, there is some higher power that can at least help to solve the problem. I don't think God intends things to happen or dictates our lives because we have the resources we need to live decent lives. It is a matter of generosity and of taking care of your own problems before trying to deal with someone else's. Because if you choose to either deal with or ignore someone else's problems, you still have your own to deal with. If you choose to deal with your own problems first, it will only strengthen your ability to deal with someone else's.

The reason I want to be a brain surgeon is because I have always been fascinated with anatomy—not just human anatomy. When I was younger, I used to operate on mice, birds, and frogs. I would just cut right into them. When I was ten, my turtle died. We buried him for a little while, but then I dug him back up because I wanted to see what was inside of him. He had been buried and his shell had just fallen off, so

I still had to cut his bones. It is more than just being fascinated by the insides of things or cutting into the core of things, it is really about preserving the mind. I've always liked smart people and I'd like to help them stay smart.

I have a younger sister and we get along okay. We just have normal sibling battles. She goes to a different school than I do. I am proud of her and I encourage her to be a strong individual. I think in some sibling relationships, especially when they are of the same gender and very close in age, there can be an unhealthy symbiosis that happens. I love her and she is my sister, but I will always encourage her to be independent and to do the things that are the most interesting to her and only to her.

I don't really know where I'd like to end up living. For a long time I wanted to live in Brazil. I had been looking through this book that my mom's friend had brought over. I saw this picture of a house on the bank of a river and I decided that I wanted to build my own house in Brazil on the bank of a river. I'd want my house by a river because I like water so much. It's so gentle and lyrical. I never want to get married and have kids, and I know I'm only thirteen, but I feel like getting married and having a family means worrying about a lot of people. I watch and listen to my parents, and I know that you can't be selfish in a family or marriage situation. I am mostly concerned with doing right by myself at this point. I'll probably change my mind, but right now it's not even remotely appealing to me.

There are more than a few ways to be smart in this world. In addition to many other theories, there has always been the conventional academicians and then the people who just have a certain awareness. But I think I'm a combination of both. I tend to have an overview of the world that doesn't really fit into any category of intelligence. It's just the way I see things. I know that there are young black kids out there today, both boys and girls, who are doing things and behaving in ways that are eating them up inside. They feel like they have nowhere to turn. To those I would say: Find something you can do that feels good, that you know feels good and that *is* good, and keep doing it.

I feel lucky that I have somewhere to turn. But mostly I feel lucky that if all I had was myself, that would be enough.

JAMINICA

Fourteen
San Francisco, California

Kids in school have labeled me as black because I am vocal and opinionated. Nobody can really make me feel a way that's going to make me not say what I am going to say, but that kind of label—which I assume is made to make me feel that being black bears the curse of loudness and maybe I oughta do something about changing that fact—is effectively hurtful. I let it get to me if it needs to, like if I really feel there's a reason I'm hearing it. Otherwise I just try to ignore it.

When I was in the third grade I took ballet and the teacher, who was white, hated me. She was just mean. I know that my name is difficult to pronounce, but it's not that difficult, and after a month of being in the class, she still couldn't remember how to say it. She couldn't actually remember it at all. She didn't take the time to remember my name and that made me mad. She didn't take the time because I was the only black girl in the class and she didn't want to know my name. I got an ulcer because of the stress I felt to perform for that woman and to be known and remembered by her. The doctors were bewildered that a seven-year-old would have so much stress. Pretty soon I decided I wasn't going to be a ballerina.

The other girls in my class were all very supportive. I remember not being able to do a cartwheel when the class first started, and they were always encouraging me. By the time I left the class, I could do a cartwheel and they all clapped. I also remember being in *The Nutcracker*, which I loved and felt so proud about. I had lots of ideas about being a great ballerina until I got sick. I was determined, but not so determined that I could withstand a racist ballet teacher who gave me an ulcer.

I carry that memory of my ballet teacher with me every day only because I can't get rid of it. What brings me peace of mind, what I do for myself, is to take little steps to get through the day and to remember who is there when I need help. The fact that I can do both of these things on a day-to-day basis is the reinforcing element in my life. Sometimes I feel weary, but I also feel like I have some control over my moods. I can wake up in the morning and know that my mood is going to try and control me that day, but if I focus hard enough, I can change that.

I love reading. I like Shakespeare a lot. I'm reading *The Odyssey* in English, which is hard to mix with Shakespeare at the moment. But my favorite book of all time is *I Know Why the Caged Bird Sings* by Maya Angelou. I read that book in seventh grade and then twice more after that. Her voice seemed to, like, echo through me. The way she describes things, you know she feels every word she puts on the page. I knew what I was reading when I read that book; I could see the people in her life and I could relate to her experiences. During one incident in the book, she has to go to the dentist because her tooth is rotting and the dentist told her he couldn't take her tooth out because she is black. I saw her experience with the dentist so vividly in my mind and I immediately felt like if she could go through that sort of thing and come out on top, then I could too.

What I like about Shakespeare, who is so different from someone like Maya Angelou, is that he is clear in another way. He has his own honesty and incredible respect for love and romance. I don't really think I'm a romantic, but I have a good imagination, and Shakespeare's writing is perfect for someone with a good imagination.

My main struggle and focus these days is to do my homework, do it well, and make good grades. I keep to myself a lot, not because I'm antisocial at all, but because of the energy it takes to have really good, trusting friendships. I have one good white girlfriend and a couple of good black girlfriends. I don't differentiate the trust factor between my black and white friends—it's hard to trust anyone. But it is also sort of strange when my white girlfriend asks me about something I do or like and then she'll say, "Is that what all black people do or like?" And I tell her, "Well, it's what I do, but I can't tell you if every black person on the planet does it, too." It seems to me sometimes that white people are fascinated by black people, as if we were a separate species altogether only to be observed but never known.

There is the one side, which represents people like my ballet teacher who was loath to remember my name and felt that if she kept ignoring me I would disappear—which I did. And then there's the other side, which represents those people who sort of ogle and wonder with these looks on their faces that say, "Ooooh, how strange and exciting!" I've known some white girls who get a kind of thrill from rap music and from watching rappers on MTV but who are also afraid of black men.

You can't escape racism. It's everywhere, and that's not a negative or pessimistic comment. Racism *is* everywhere. We'll do a lot better if we identify that fact so we can try and move on. I don't know how to make people understand this more clearly. I have enough trouble understanding it for myself, so I don't actually think I need to know how to make everyone understand this. Still, if I'm the one who's experiencing racism, isn't it important to let people know of that experience? It's kind of a no-win situation, I guess.

In terms of the way I view myself relative to my peers, those who are my friends as well as those who are not, both black and white, I'm not that concerned with the way I look or dress. I think I'm probably all right looking and I like to do different things with my hair because it's fun. But I think the more you worry about the way you look, the more susceptible you are to being insecure and getting your feelings hurt. In the long run, it doesn't really matter. In the short run, I'm not saying that I haven't wished I was this or that; I don't think I'd be normal if I didn't. I'm just saying in theory I don't think the way a person looks should matter. What happens when I look in the mirror is an entirely different thing.

Like I said, I try to stay focused on my studies. I enjoy school and learning. I don't look anywhere else to learn what I need to know for when I get out in the world. I think that as a teenager, my world is basically school and my family and friends. I think school is in its own way a very small representative of the way people treat each other in the world, both black and white, boys and girls, teachers and students. If you pay attention, you start to understand that most of it is about power.

I will never have the luxury of knowing what it's like to not be branded in society. I read somewhere once that young white girls lose their self-esteem around this age and that black girls don't, which is kind of weird, since black girls have so much more to deal with. Maybe it's because we have so much to deal with that we don't want to risk giving up our self-esteem because then we'd really be in trouble. We'd still have all the issues we have to negotiate with no self-esteem. Sounds grim. I'm not saying that I've got this huge amount of self-esteem; I'm saying that what amount I do have is mine.

I can't actually do or be anything other than what I do and be. Unless you want to get into a big activist battle, you accept the stereotypes given to you and just try and reshape them along the way. So in a way, this gives me a lot of freedom. I can't be looked at as any worse in society than I already am—black and female is pretty high on the list of things not to be. The freedom of it is, I am black and female, yes, but I am also many other things and have the ability to be even more.

ALAZA

Seventeen
Portland, Oregon

I think I noticed the difference between blacks and whites when I was in grade school, which was integrated, but the white teachers never called on the black kids and treated us like we didn't know the answers. I didn't say anything then, but if it were now, I would definitely confront the issue: If someone thinks I'm dumb, then I need to talk with them about that.

It doesn't occur to me so much that being black in America is this huge struggle, but I'll tell you, being gay in the black community is a trip. There are not a lot of black girls in my community who are gay or who are willing to admit they are gay. And it definitely seems to me that the white community is much more tolerant of gay people than the black community. I came out when I was fifteen and it was a totally instinctive thing; it just felt comfortable to me. All the relationships I had been in with boys lacked something and I couldn't really put my finger on what it was. The first time I was with a girl, I knew what that something was, but I still can't really explain it. I'm not gonna front, you know. I think boys are cute and all, but I wouldn't want to talk to them or have a relationship with them.

In a way, I think that women are more trustworthy than men, but I also know that women can be just as untrustworthy as men. I think I feel safer with women in terms of being emotional with them. The woman I'm with now is black and she's older. She's twenty-three. I'm totally in love for the first time. I've only been with a couple of other girls before her. At first, my mother and my family thought I was just going through a phase, but now they know I'm for real. The way I deal with judgmentalism around this issue is by being myself and knowing that I am loving another person because she is being herself, too. I think I'm old enough to make my own decisions. I know how to take care of myself.

Before I came out, I was homophobic just like everybody else I was hanging around with. I didn't know that the feeling I was missing with guys was the feeling I was going to find with girls. And even when I did realize, the first girl I started liking sort of repulsed me because she acted so masculine. I was like, "Gross! You actin' like a boy!" Her hair was real short and she acted like a man. I know that a lot of homosexual and lesbian relationships may seem like they are trying to simulate heterosexual relationships and a lot of them do. I was in a relationship like that before, but it felt too restrictive. The woman I'm with now is kind of like me; she's not too feminine (I think it's boring when women are too feminine) and she's not too masculine. She is just herself. We both are.

Being in love is the bomb. We argue and stuff, but we always work it out within like three minutes because we can't stand to be angry with each other. We talk about having a family and she's decided that not only is it going to be me who gets pregnant, but the father *definitely* has to be a brother. And that's fine with me—I want to have kids. I wouldn't get pregnant with a white dude because I want my child to be black. I know that mixed kids are considered black or half black or whatever, but chile, I want my baby to be *black* black. If I really think about it and it turned out that I couldn't find a decent brother or had to adopt for some reason, then I know that the color wouldn't really matter. But if I have my choice, the baby's gonna be black.

My circle of friends are all gay. I don't even think I have one straight friend left. Our roommate was straight before she moved in with me and my girlfriend. But my family is straight, straight and then some. My mother drives the city bus and has for years. She's had her problems, but she's doing well now. My oldest brother is twenty-six and he moved out when he was fourteen. He just works and lives with his girlfriend. My oldest sister is thirty and she is by far the best example of us all: She graduated from high school *and* college, she's married and lives with her husband, she doesn't have any babies (so you *know* she's goin' somewhere!), and she has a good job. Then I have another sister who is twenty-four and she lives with friends. And then another brother, who is twenty-one, and he's in prison for murder. I had another brother too, but he got shot five years ago when he was fifteen. He had gotten into a fight with another boy, and the other boy shot him, and that was it. My brother died on a street corner with a whole lot of people looking at him. He laid there for about an hour before the ambulance came.

The story that I have about my brother who's in prison (although I've never really heard the whole story) is that he was selling drugs and some woman tried to rip him off and he accidentally shot her. His friends say that he did it. My brother won't say anything and can't really anyway because the phones are bugged inside, so I don't know whether he actually did it or not. His actions have had a strong impact on my life, though, and I think the whole gang and drug scene is dumb. After he joined the gang he was in before he went to prison, everything that happened in his life was bad: His friends got shot, he never held a job, and it has all ended in a life sentence in prison. You can't stop people from doing what they're gonna do, and I'm not sure I'll ever know what has so far stopped me from choosing a dangerous life like he did. I guess I just realize that I have a choice. There is a lot of pain for my brother now and for those of us who care about him. If I hadn't seen what had happened to him, I still probably would have made the same choices I've made in my life. You just can't play around with your life like that.

My girlfriend sells drugs for a living. She used to be in a gang, but she left it when we met. I told her it was too stupid, that she was smarter than that. I can't get her to stop selling drugs, but at least she's out of the gang, and all of her buyers or their messengers come to the house; she never leaves the house to stay out of shooting range. Plus, she knows I worry about her, so she don't need to be going anywhere. If we need milk, I'll go. We met at a get-together at a mutual friend's house last summer. She was recovering from having gotten shot in the leg. We hit it off right away and I nursed her back to health, you know, and she left the gang and everything. I know selling drugs is bad, but I must say, I do like the money. She can't do anything else just now because there's a warrant out for her arrest, but she's trying to take care of that so she can get a legitimate job.

I'm not willing to risk my life for the money, but I love her enough to risk my life by being around her. She's slowing up lately, though, really. She's been doing a lot less business lately. I can't tell her what to do; all I can do is show her that I value my life and I hope she'll value hers. I think that's what love is all about; when you realize that someone cares about you and you are worthy of their love, then you start to take care of yourself a little better. That's why she left the gang.

I'm the first girl she's ever been with. But she's never been pregnant and she's twenty-three. She's been shot, but she hasn't been pregnant. I'd rather have a baby than get shot any day. I know they both hurt and I know that the chances of either or both happening are pretty good. But if I had my choice, I'd rather get pregnant. I think my girlfriend hasn't gotten pregnant because she spent her early years hard-core gangin' and she didn't have no time to be messin' around with nobody. It's kind of a miracle, though, now that I think about it. Besides, I know she wouldn't be tryin' to go on no-body's welfare. First of all, her mother would end up taking care of the baby and her mother sells drugs, too. My girlfriend likes to do things the way she likes to do them. Welfare wouldn't be enough money for her anyway.

I want to be a singer. I sing all the time, and the other night I sang in front of an audience of about three hundred at this record release party. It felt so good. It's taken me a little while to get into the idea of performing because usu-ally I just open my mouth and the words just flow right out and I don't have to do anything else. But the other night, when people were watching me, clapping, singing, and yell-ing, "Go on, girl! Sing it!" You know I did. My main job for the time being, now that I've moved in with my girlfriend and am paying rent, is at Popeye's Chicken. Minimum Wage. But I work a lot of hours, so I do all right.

My girlfriend loves to brag about my singing. I just wrapped a duet with a local artist that'll be coming out soon. I think the label we recorded on is local too, but it feels so good to be in the recording studio. I write songs, but I don't write music. I work with some musicians because I'm trying to put a tape of my own together. I'll write songs and then come to the studio and hum it to them, and they can recreate what I'm humming on their instruments. Singing is like the best high in the world to me. I know I'm gonna keep singing.

I've still got another eight credits to finish before I can get my high-school diploma and I'm not really thinking about college. If I ever did go to college, though, it would be a cosmetology school because I want to learn how to put makeup on dead people. I would like to be the person who makes dead people look cute. I've been to a lot of funerals and the dead people always look so bad. They never look like themselves; they're all gray and everything. I'd be thinking, *You know, they coulda done their hair different, too.* I've lost a lot of friends. And, like I said, I lost my brother. I think when you leave this world, you oughta be looking cute.

I never think about my own looks really, or my body, or anything like that. I never worry about being beautiful for my girlfriend. I mean, I keep my nails nice, and clothes are a lot of fun, and I do what I can with my hair, but that's about it. I've never felt envious toward white girls about the way they look. It's irrelevant to me. In fact, when I was in a more integrated school as a child and had some white girl-friends, I remember they used to be jealous of my hair because I could do so many things with it. I think when I was younger, I was very shy and kind of quiet, which I know is hard to believe since I'm pretty loud now. But then when I turned maybe fourteen, I just knew that I *had* to feel good about myself, that I couldn't feel bad about myself and survive. Plus, I can feel in my singing that I have always had a voice inside of me that wants to keep coming.

I've never felt inferior to anybody. It's not in me. I re-member some of the white girls from middle school talking about how they wish they had the same kind of style, atti-tude, and sense of humor I have. I remember saying, "Yeah, girl. It's good to be black." And it is.

MYESHA

Twelve
Cambridge, Massachusetts

I lived in a small city outside Los Angeles until I was ten. We lived in a mostly black neighborhood—maybe three quarters black—and the school I went to was the same. So when I was younger, I didn't think that being black meant being different. When we moved East and my neighborhood was the reverse—three quarters white—that's when I started to think being black meant being different because I was. I had some white friends in California, but not too many. I have a friend at school now who is white but who doesn't hardly know any other white people because she lives in a black neighborhood. All her friends are black, which I guess is okay, as long as she realizes who she is.

I think most of who I am is about my race. Being black means that I am proud and that I read and study a lot about my history because I don't hardly learn anything in school about black history, I have to teach myself or have my parents teach me. That means I have to know what to ask them, though, and it means taking the responsibility of learning about the kinds of effect history has had on the present. I told my teacher one time that I wanted to learn a little more about my history and that everyone else should learn as much about black history as we do about white history, and she told me that she had taught black history last year and this year she wanted to teach something else.

I miss California because of the support a strong black community gives, but it wasn't like when I moved here I was nervous about seeing white people. Up until the time I came here, no white people had said or done anything to me that would make me feel nervous. Since I've been here, I have experienced the feeling of being an outcast, which does make me feel nervous and uncomfortable. Sometimes at school I'll get into an argument with a couple of white girls, and the two of them will gang up on me because they are both white, which to them means they have something I don't and never will. Usually the way I respond to a situation like that is by telling them that they can be white all they want, but I'm proud to be black. They think that because they're white, then they're right. Being black doesn't make me wrong, as much as people might like to think it does. I usually don't tell my parents when that kind of thing happens, not because I think they won't understand, but more because I don't want them to feel bad. My dad has always told me that my life is going to be hard first because I'm black and second because I'm a woman. The reason I know that blacks keep having it hard is because we've never had a black president. And we've also never had a female president. I guess people must think that the combination of black and female must be pretty threatening to a lot of people.

Just because there are more white kids than black kids at my school, it doesn't mean that I feel bad about myself or that I don't feel as pretty as the white girls. Comparing myself to anyone else doesn't feel right to me anyway. As far as boys go, if I like him, I like him, no matter what race he is. But still, even though it doesn't feel right to compare myself to the white girls, it is really hard not to. I have white girlfriends, but I don't really trust them. Sometimes they act like my friends, and sometimes they leave me out and act like they're not my friends at all. They'll call me names behind my back. Sometimes I tell the principal rather than talk directly to the girls because they get the same idea about ganging up on me because they're all white and I'm not. I don't need their acceptance or their approval, and if they try to make me feel bad on purpose, then I just try and ignore them. I'm not sure how much of the way they act is about me being black, but I think it could be more about my being black than I actually know or understand. I don't even know if they understand how racist they can act.

Last year I had to change out of a class because some white girls kept bothering me. There were only two other black kids in that class out of twenty, and my teacher was white too. Now I'm in a class where there are six other black kids, so I guess that's an improvement. I like school a lot, though. I love math, science, and music. I never feel intimidated about liking science. I want to be a scientist when I grow up because I like the idea of curing people. There are a lot of resources in the world that we haven't even begun to discover, like in the rain forest there are certain flowers that contain healing components in them. There are ways to research and experiment in the rain forest without destroying it; we just need to be more careful. We can't be using up the trees in the rain forest for things like paper; we have plenty of paper here to recycle. I think that being a scientist and finding cures for diseases is one of the best things that a human being can do.

I think the strongest force behind who I am is my parents. I know that I will be able to do a lot in life but that I have to pay attention and keep learning. My parents help me every day. My whole family, both here and in California, are smart and proud people. Family means a lot to me because they have always been there for me. I'll probably have a family of my own one day, but I have a long way to go before I start thinking about that. I think that when we see young black girls on the news who are pregnant, or have lots of babies, or are on welfare, it's because the people who have power in the media aren't interested in showing anything positive about black people. All I can say about teen pregnancy is that I wouldn't want to be in that position. I think sometimes girls get pregnant to be rebellious and sometimes they do it to make themselves feel important, even though they probably end up feeling worse. Even though we don't see a lot of positive black images in the media, I read a lot of positive things about black people and my dad is always showing me articles or telling me about some black brain surgeon or someone.

I love reading. Right now I'm reading a novel about a black boy who moves to a white neighborhood and how he has to live with all this discrimination, like getting rocks thrown through his window and having people spray-paint signs on his locker at school like NIGGER GO HOME! Nothing like that has ever happened to me. When we first moved here, there were some white girls who used to call my house and bother me, but then my mom got on the phone and told them, "Excuse me, don't be calling *my* house!" I'm very proud of my mom. I like that she is strong and can get through things. I admire both my mom and dad a lot. They have been really positive role models for me.

I don't really read or look at fashion magazines. Sometimes I look at *Essence* or *Ebony,* and I only get to watch MTV once in a while. I think most rap artists are just trying to make money and don't care what it takes to make it, even if they need to use women in a negative way. I like the girl rap group TLC, but I don't really look up to them or anything. I know that they are making it for themselves and trying to put something out there that is positive, but some of the things they sing about are not necessary. They don't need to be singing about sex; people know about sex already. I think making money is okay and being popular is okay too, but knowing who you are and being responsible is more important than both money and popularity combined.

I go to church sometimes. We went to church much more when we were in California, but we haven't been able to find a church out here that we like. I do believe in God. My grandmother has taught me a lot about God and the spirituals. I'm not sure I believe all of it; I mean, it's not like anyone has gotten a letter from God lately. But because tradition and the history of God is important to my family and because I value history, I believe in God.

The thing about black history, or slave history, that sticks out most in my mind is a story that my dad told me about how when all of the Africans were being brought over on ships to America to be sold as slaves, if a ship ever got too heavy, the white people would tie black babies to strings and dangle them overboard for the sharks to eat. That kind of inhumane action is so awful to think about. Black people have always been as smart and as strong as white people, maybe even stronger. I don't have to remind myself of that strength; I just know it. When I think about all those babies who were killed because of white people's mean and igno-rant ways, and all the evil of slavery, in a way, as painful as it is, I feel even more proud that we have gone through so much as a people and are still here. And you know, we've been very good about all this, don't you think? I mean, we could really be a lot more angry than we are. I remember telling that story about the slave babies on the ship to my class, and the teacher said it sounded terrible and then just moved on really quick. The rest of the kids just sat there with their jaws hanging open. I don't know if they believed me or not. A couple of them laughed.

People who say blacks need to move on and stop talking

about our history probably wouldn't say the same thing if we were all talking about white history. In fact, we talk about white history all the time nonstop. I have a couple of black friends at school, and we do talk about being black, and what we want to be when we grow up, and how we want to make changes in the world. And we talk about boys, clothes, and of course hair. We talk about girl stuff, but we're not so self-conscious about the way we look that we'd ever worry about breaking a nail or anything.

I guess I just don't think too much about whether I am pretty or not. I like having brown skin. I have wondered what it would be like to have white skin, and I think it would be helpful for white people to wonder about having black skin every now and again, but I've never wanted to have white skin. And blue eyes are pretty, but not for me. I like my hair whether I straighten it or not. It's my hair and I can wear it the way I want to.

I sure hope there is more than one way of being black because if I had to be black like other black people, then I wouldn't be myself. I know that there are black people who behave in a way that makes them think they are representing the best way to be black or the coolest way to be black, but I think the best way for me to be black is for me to be myself. I don't judge other people. If I judge people by telling them they can't do or say something the way they are doing it, then I am putting limitations on them as well as on myself. I think there are a whole lot of ways to be black and to be Myesha is one of them.

SOPHIE

Twenty
Freehold, New Jersey

I was two or three when I was adopted into a white family. I don't remember exactly. The only time I heard or learned anything about my birthparents was when my daughter was born three months ago and I needed to find out some information about my medical history. I found out the name of my birthmother, but nothing about my birthfather. I have never been interested in looking into it further. I don't know the woman who gave me up; why not let her decision lie?

At first I didn't think about my color. But then when people in school started asking me why I didn't "act" black, I realized that I was different. My parents have never said anything to me about being black or different. Never. In high school there were other black girls, the "sisters," as they called themselves, and they would say things behind my back about how I thought I was better than them or how I acted weird or snobby. I was crushed. I got all revved up over something I couldn't understand. I couldn't understand why they would be mean to me when I never did anything mean to them.

In the very beginning of high school, I was never drawn to those girls. In real honesty, my parents had actually taught me to fear black people. We were never around black people when I was growing up, although there was this friend of my father who was this really big, jolly black guy. He was married to a white woman and brought her with him to the house. I remember thinking, *This is great. It's no big deal having black people and white people in families together; people must do this all the time.* Then for some reason he suddenly stopped coming over and we never heard about him again. My mom and I saw his wife in the grocery store one time and my mom just ignored her. My mom didn't say anything about it, which I immediately interpreted as meaning the interracial thing was actually not okay at all.

For the rest of my childhood and into my teens, I grew up around upper-middle-class white people. I don't just mean any old white, I mean yacht club white. And that was a very confusing experience. When my two older brothers and my older sister and I started going to the yacht club to

111

hang out—I was probably eleven around then—I went thinking that I was just like them. I knew nothing about black history, had never even heard of Martin Luther King, and denied my image in the mirror. In fact, if I could help it, I didn't look in the mirror at all because I was afraid of what I saw. I didn't think the color of my skin matched up with who I was. Of course my mother was constantly telling me to wear the khaki pants, the Northern Isle sweaters, and you know—"Buffy and Bif, here we come!" None of it made any sense to me at all, particularly when I arrived at the yacht club tennis courts with my racket in hand and everyone looked at me like I was from another planet.

My parents divorced when I was about eight, and so me and my brothers and sister lived with my mom from then on. After a few more strange experiences at the yacht club and observing the way my family viewed black people as if they were looking down on them from some sort of ivory tower, I asked my mom why I was here in this family with them. She said, "Your father wanted you. He thought it would be nice to give somebody a better chance in life." And I was like, "Great, I have this better chance in life, but I'm in hell." Then I started losing it. Grade school and middle school were mostly very private and very white, but when I went to a public high school, where there were even black teachers, I experienced a turning point. I instigated my being black completely on my own and felt fairly safe in doing it. I had slowly reached this point where I felt being black as a concept was okay. That was a good start.

After that first step of accepting what being black *could* mean for me, the rest was about undoing the fear my parents had instilled in me. That was hard. I had to undo their classist and elitist ways of thinking. It just sort of hit me one day when this black girl came up to me at school and just started talking to me. She had been one of the girls who had talked about me behind my back, but somehow, all of a sudden, we were just standing there talking and it was fine. We were human beings.

I think I may have dated two white boys at the most, but it felt weird. I didn't need to suffer the potential humiliation of being rejected by a white boy after having felt so humiliated in my family. I knew that I could be and do something else. I was sixteen when I had my first real boyfriend and he was black. My mother almost had a heart attack when I brought him home. She couldn't believe I would choose "this" after the way she had tried to raise me. My boyfriend would come to the house with me, and my mom would say hello in passing and then leave the room. She never had a single conversation with him or me except to exhibit her disapproval.

My siblings were no help; I never related to them. For so many years I looked out of myself and into their world trying to find me. All I saw in their world was what I was supposed to be. I tried and tried to fit into their mold, nearly killed myself trying, but it never worked. We just fought and fought. They were not interested in understanding what I was going through and I didn't know how to tell them. So I sort of became—what my mother referred to me as—a hermit. At the time, I was devastated that she would call me that, but she was right. I'd go to school, come home, get something to eat and take it up to my room, do my homework, maybe make a brief appearance at dinner, and then go back upstairs and go to bed. That was my way of dealing, or not dealing, as it was. I felt so stuck. I had no freedom; I couldn't go anywhere. I started feeling terrified that this was what my life was going to look like forever.

In school, though, my life was different. After I started feeling comfortable having black friends and had a black boyfriend, I felt that I was onto something. I was carving a path out of what I felt was a binding and hellish situation at home so that I could make my way as the person I felt I was instinctively. But still, at first it was hard. Nothing came easily. I spent a lot of time feeling not black enough. It was such an extreme for me to think, and in some ways, be forced to feel, like a white person and wanting like crazy to make my skin color dissappear to not feeling like my skin color was dark enough and wanting to be accepted as black.

I remember going to my boyfriend's house. He lived in a very urban, lower-class neighborhood, while I had come from a very rural, upper-class neighborhood. His house was run-down and I remember thinking at first, *This is how* they *live*. I could smack myself now for thinking that, but at the time I was making a direct pit stop from ducks, plaid, BMWs, and argyle. What was I to make of this seemingly poverty-stricken sight that was my boyfriend's house? His mother was the most wonderful person, and she and I became very close. She was like a surrogate black mother to me. My boyfriend and I were together for about two years, and I ended up spending a lot of time at that run-down house, which eventually felt so much softer, lived-in, and homey than my own house. I learned from my boyfriend's mother that you can live in a box and still be happy. She had created a certain quality of life that had nothing to do with material wealth or status.

That experience made me think about what my mother had said to me when I asked her about being adopted and she had told me about this "better way"—that is, the white way—and yet I felt no quality of life. And here was this woman, living a far less fortunate life than me and my family lived, who was happy as a clam. For most of my life, I hated my father. When he got remarried to a younger woman and started a newer family, I was fuming for months. I was, like, "Okay, this man wants to give me a better way? He brought me into this white house, this white world, and then he left. He left me in a place I didn't want to be and where nobody else wanted me to be." I saw no reason to like him.

But, as we almost always do with our parents, I did finally reach a point where I at least did not hate him. This point came around the time I got my driver's license. I remember my mother being so scared about me getting my license because she thought I was going to get it, get a car, get the keys, and get out. I of course found her fear very perplexing since she had wanted me to get out for a long time before then anyway. I remember thinking, *This is really something. This woman has tried to push me out of myself and into her mold, has said so many hurtful things to me without even knowing it, and she wanted me to stick around and be part of her life? No thanks.* I thought she was nuts. When I graduated from high school, I got my license, and my dad gave me a car and some money for an apartment, and that was it. I was out. My dad giving me a car wasn't such a big deal since he owned a dealership and gave all of the kids cars when we got our licenses, but his gesture with the money for an apartment seemed sort of human on his part. I felt like he might have understood that I really just needed to be on my own.

Sure enough, before long I ran into the problem of: Gee, I don't know how to take care of myself. And why would I? I had been pampered and spoiled, not because I was a good child or because my parents loved me so much, but because that is what parents with money do for their kids. I knew nothing about budgeting or paying bills. All I knew how to do was escape. Luckily my boyfriend at the time, who I had been with since my senior year of high school and who I married five months ago, was with me through all of the trial and error. He has helped me so much to become the person I am today. I think I would still be stuck in my bedroom at my mother's house if it wasn't for him.

My husband is black. We are very close. We talk about everything all the time. There have been some real rocky parts in our relationship, but I think that has been because of me mostly and what I have grown up thinking—not just in terms of race, but also after my mother was divorced, she was constantly on this male-bashing trip. She was always saying, "There is no true love, there is no true love." She said it like a mantra. But I definitely picked up on it and the idea stayed with me for a long time.

When I was pregnant with my daughter I was so scared that she was going to come out too dark because my husband is very dark. In my head, I still thought I needed to produce a white baby for my mother and my family in order for them to accept her. As soon as my daughter was born, though, all of those ideas vanished. All I thought was that she was the most beautiful thing I had ever seen in my life. Because I am adopted, the biological connection of giving birth to a child is sometimes almost too much for me to describe without losing it and bursting into tears. My daughter's birth has been the best thing that has ever happened to me. She is a miracle. She really is.

It has been much easier to spend time with my family lately because I have my own family now. When I'm at family functions, I make pretty for the camera and let all of the stares and the snickers roll off my back because I know I'm only visiting and will be able to leave very soon. The damage to my identity will always be with me. I feel thankful that I have been able to transcend the pain enough so that I can be responsible and loving toward my child. My daughter will grow up learning about her black culture and heritage first, but she will also learn about many other cultures, too. I want her to understand that one set of her grandparents are white and that white culture has something to offer her. But this child is part of *my* family, not anybody else's. I hope that she will grow up culturally well-rounded, but mainly, above all, I want her to grow up feeling constant love. There's no way of knowing where I would be if my parents had not adopted me, and for that, I am grateful to them. I have been able to make a life for myself that feels right, and perhaps I might not have been able to do that if I hadn't been adopted.

Yes, my life is my own and, I'll tell you, it is the most amazing thing in the world for me to wake up in the morning and look into my baby's crib and see this little brown face looking back up at me, a face I can see myself in. There is no greater feeling. Finally.

NADINE

Fifteen
Roxbury, Massachusetts

When I was thirteen years old, I decided that I'd like to do some experimenting with makeup. So I went to this huge CVS, which had a fairly decent-sized cosmetics section, and looked for some makeup to try on. None of the foundations, blushes, or eyeshadows matched my skin tone. I thought for a minute about asking one of the salespeople for help, but it didn't take long before I realized that there was no makeup for black people there. I didn't pursue it further.

My parents fled from Haiti when I was three or four. My father was Lucien Mallebranch. He was very involved in the political climate during the time that Duvalier was in office. And my mother was Jacqueline Adrien. They are both deceased. My father died of a cancer-related disease and my mother died of causes unknown. My social worker has told me recently that she has some new information on my mother's death, but I'm not ready to hear it yet. I have two older sisters who stayed in Haiti, and a younger brother and sister who live in a foster home in Florida. When my parents brought our family to the States, they moved us to Florida. We lived in an all-black, poverty-stricken neighborhood in a town called Immokaly, which wasn't at all what we had been accustomed to. By Haitian standards, my father was an important figurehead and we were able to live very comfortably in Haiti. When we moved here, my father was not prepared for what he faced. His expectations of making a happy life for us here came crashing down. Because he didn't have a degree or a document verifying his work and high-standing position in Haiti, he ended up having to get a job as a dishwasher at a hotel. We had to eat.

I went to kindergarten through fourth grade at a school where there were kids from all ethnic backgrounds: Asian, Hispanic, white, black. But I had a very difficult time feeling comfortable with any of the kids at school. I felt upheaved and I wasn't a very trusting child. The neighborhood we were living in was so foreign to me that I think I carried that same sense of the unfamiliar with me to school. Also, our family life had changed in the way we all related to each other. In Haiti, I remember my father and I as being very close, which was unusual for a Haitian father. Normally in Haiti fathers are not especially close with their daughters. When we moved to the States, I sometimes didn't see my father for weeks at a time. He would be at work until long after I had gone to bed, asleep when I left for school, and gone again when I got home. I was no longer his "little princess" as I had been in Haiti, which deeply affected me.

At that time, my brother, who is four years younger than me, and I didn't really have any kind of sibling relationship because he was so much younger. My baby sister hadn't even been born yet. I haven't seen my brother in five years and have no contact at all with my sister. It's not that I don't want to see them, but between moving around from foster home to foster home and focusing on getting through school, I don't think it's a good idea right now for us to be in close contact. My situation is too unstable.

After my father died, my mom also became sick. She was pregnant with my little sister when she first became ill, and her illness eventually became so bad that she couldn't care for my brother and me. She gave birth to my sister and then put her and my brother in foster care while arranging for me to move up north to live with my aunt in Boston. I lived with my aunt for a while, but it was not the best situation. She was both emotionally and verbally abusive, and I knew enough to know that I would not be able to move forward with my life if I stayed with her. So then I moved into a shelter-type place for thirty days until a foster home became available. And that's where I've lived up until about three days ago when I moved into another foster home with a woman who I feel more compatible with.

As you can see, there was a lot going on for me before I could afford the time to think about being black and female in America. The irony is that when I did start thinking about it, I didn't exactly know what I was supposed to think. I mean, being from Haiti and having a sense of its history as the first independent black nation in the Western hemisphere, I *knew* that I was black. It was not an issue in Haiti, where everyone was black and there was integrity in that fact. When we moved here, I very quickly realized that in America, being black was another story. It hit me hard, too. Because here, it is an issue that far exceeds just being in the minority; there are serious power differentials and excrutiatingly painful historical facts to reconcile.

When I was still in Florida growing up in my neighborhood there, I remember wondering why I had to be black. Like, *Why me?* My complexion seemed too dark and my nose seemed too wide. I wished desperately that I could be white so that I could go back to the lifestyle we had known in Haiti. Being black in America meant being poor. It wasn't until one of my teachers in the fourth grade, Mrs. Brown—oh, I loved her!—said to me, "Girl, there is nothing wrong with you, there never was, and I pray to God there never will be! Take a good look in the mirror, chile, you are beautiful!" And I started looking in the mirror a little more and slowly began to reach a point where I could tell myself that I wasn't horrible looking anyway.

When I moved to Boston, I attended a public junior high school, which was predominantly black, with a few whites and Cambodians. My first year was a lot of peer pressure, just like any junior high experience: a lot of hype, trend-setting and -following, stuff like that. I never got the feeling that the school had any particular concern about academics; it was more about social activities and making friends. I couldn't see getting all worked up about trends, although I did have straightened hair. This natural hair that I have now is only a year old. It keeps me more focused, at least in the sense of being 100 percent black and female, not some watered-down, assimilated version. When I had my hair straightened, it was more an issue of management, according to the adults in my life. And I just kept it that way until a year ago when I got tired of my hair breaking off from the damage caused by continuous processing.

Because I am from Haiti, I think it is interesting to contemplate whether or not I have a stronger, and perhaps more peaceful, sense of my African heritage than most African-Americans do. I think that I am more at ease with the part of me that claims my Haitian history than I am with the part of me that claims my American history. Haitians are a do-for-self culture, and coming to America and finding out the horror and submission of slave history has sort of gnawed around the edges of my soul. Seeing so clearly that black Americans are still not considered as "beautiful" or "smart" or "good" as white Americans is completely unsettling. As a fifteen-year-old black girl in this society, I can flip through page after page of any major fashion magazine and not once see myself. What I do see is women who look nothing like me. After I have bought the magazine and flipped through it, I feel cheated and humiliated for paying the money and for believing that I might see an image I could relate to. And why do I have to buy *Essence* and *Ebony* in order to see an image of celebrated blackness? It's unfair. By default, I feel compelled to go and work for one of those mainstream fashion magazines, on behalf of black girls and women everywhere, to try and make some changes. But I really resent having to be pushed to that point.

A couple of years after my ill-fated search for makeup is when I happened upon *Essence* and *Ebony* for the first time. I was probably thirteen at the time, and I remember feeling this strange and very new feeling of hope about the way I looked. I was so thrilled to see black women on the cover, but I was also angry that I had waited so long. The pain and insecurity I endured prior to this discovery made my awakening bittersweet.

Fortunately for me, my father, when he was alive, was very interested in feeding the mind history and literature. So my early years were filled with Haitian cultural philosophies. When I came here, all I learned about black culture in America was that black people were slaves, and then Martin Luther King showed up and single-handedly freed us all! So I had to self-educate. I spent a lot of time at the library and found out about people like Malcolm X, Nat Turner, Sojourner Truth, and Denmark Vessey. I realized how hard black people had fought against the nature of the grain in this country. That was my renaissance, which left me with a sense of wanting to fight. And I have, every step of the way.

Sometimes I think about what my father accomplished in Haiti and what his family accomplished—his family is scattered throughout France now, but they were all part of Haiti's hierarchy—and I worry endlessly about living up to those accomplishments. I haven't been back to Haiti because I haven't had the means and because I haven't wanted to. I feel firmly rooted in this country right now and feel that I have a lot of work to do here. I've taken on a lot of issues that plague black America, such as the "plight of the black male." Despite the hyped-up term, I am sincerely concerned about black men in this society and the ways in which they deal with black women. I think there's a lack of understanding between black men and black women that is unnecessary, but because there are so many myths and struggles to deal with, neither black men nor black women end up getting the support they need. I think the issue is partly because black women want to be appreciated by, but not mythologized by, black men. We know we're tough, but we'd like to be pretty and soft, too. Black men have fragile egos, so they often interpret black women's needs as infringing upon their own needs. Ever since black men set foot on American soil, this country has been grinding at the black man's ego, trying to tear him down. It's all well and good to tell black men to move on, but when you're in the mire, you're breathing the stench.

I do think that young black men are far worse off than young black women because we young women have the strength of knowing that black culture has been throughout history and still is today a matriarchal one. We know that we will survive because we have. I'm also very interested in feminism and how it relates or doesn't relate, as the case may be, to black women. There is the common denominator of us all being women, which is a natural given. But from what I have read, it seems to me that when feminism began, white women wanted to get away from white men or to be equal to them. It has always been very much about these white women being given the opportunity to enter the workplace, which up until then had been a foreign concept. See, black women have *been* working. Matter of fact, we could use a vacation, come to think of it. One of the richest qualities about black culture is that when black women and black men do get along, we're not trying to be as good as each other, we're trying to be good *to* each other.

I don't spend much time thinking about my image or my body right now, but when I was younger (a little while after arriving in the States), I did have a hard time feeling okay, if you know what I mean. It has been and probably always will be to some extent an instant reflex to feel self-conscious as a black woman in this society. As I've said, there is no evidence on a consistent basis that we are beautiful, and it is not at all surprising or unrealistic to think that a character like Toni Morrison's Pecola Breedlove would go insane from wanting blue eyes. I think Pecola's character can represent young black girls in America as a whole, although perhaps on a less harsh level. It is a struggle, though, and a fine line between coming out the other side and going completely crazy.

It is bizarre when people talk about blackness as just a color and that there is no difference between black people and white people. It is precisely our skin color that fortifies and perpetuates racism in this society and, at our best moments, what makes us proud. We have to be. Without our black skin, we would be naked and our history would be more invisible than it already is.

Whether or not America wants to deal with me, I exist. And in memory of Zora: "I love myself when I am laughing."

KRISTEN

Eighteen
Washington, DC

See, I was a tomboy as a child. I was the youngest and only girl in my family, with two older brothers three and six years older. I adored my brothers. I wanted to be and play with them all the time, and most of the time they let me. My first real memory of being a girl was when I was about five or six: My brothers and I had just come in from playing basketball and were all real hot and sweaty. My brothers took their shirts off and I was, like, "Okay, I'm gonna take my shirt off, too." I was getting ready to do just that when my oldest brother said, "No! You can't do that!" And I was totally confused. I asked him why not and he said, "Because you're a girl, that's why!" Well, he had to go and get my mother to explain that one. My mother told me that I couldn't take my shirt off like them, I couldn't spit on the ground like them, and that, in fact, I couldn't be like them at all because she said, "You're a girl." Not too much of an explanation if you ask me, but she sounded serious when she said it, so I listened for the time being. Another time a couple of years later when I was playing tackle football with my brothers and their friends everyone was getting tackled except me. I was, like, "Nah, uh-uh, I don't want it like that. I want to get tackled, too!" I mean, we were playing *tackle* football. Once again, my oldest brother offered his wisdom, telling me this time that girls don't get tackled and that girls don't do that kind of stuff. I thought, *Well, what do girls do?*

I grew up in Shepherd Park in Washington, DC. The houses in my neighborhood were built in the early 1900s when the leases for their sale or rental read clearly at the top of the page: DO NOT RENT TO BLACKS. Many years later, when the city decided to desegregate the neighborhood, the officials asked the white families to stay put and most of them did. My mom and dad moved into the neighborhood about thirty years ago. So when I was growing up, the neighborhood was middle-class black and white families. In the latter years of my childhood and since then, the neighborhood has become predominantly black. I've always thought of my neighborhood as being very safe. Occasionally there would be break-ins maybe once every two years or so. All of the kids played outside and our parents knew we would be all right.

When we played outside, the girls played together and the guys played together. I was the only girl playing with the guys. We would play dirt bike tag, we skateboarded, and we played basketball. If I ever wanted to be around the girls in my neighborhood, I had to play with them separately. They never joined me in playing with the guys. So once in a while, you know, I'd go and play dolls or house or whatever with the girls. They didn't resent me and they definitely weren't jealous. I don't think they really cared.

In terms of looking at being black, my mom is very light-skinned, which sort of threw a wrench in my process of figuring stuff out. Because for the first few years of my life, I really thought she was white. I think I could recognize that there was a difference between black people and white people; lots of my extended family were light. My grandmother on my mother's side was dark and I remember asking my mom, "How can a white baby come out of a brown mommy?" Of course everyone laughed at me, but it was something that I was honestly wrestling with. My mom kept telling me that she was black, but I didn't believe her for the longest time, not until later on when I understood the way society deals with race and culture. Then I just took her word for it.

One of the other girls in my neighborhood was white. She moved to Shepherd Park when I was in the fourth grade. She was bold as me and didn't mind doing guy-type stuff. We became the best of friends. Our families got close, our mothers hung out together, and still to this day around the holidays she and her mom will come by the house with gifts and greetings. As far as having a white best friend went, I honestly didn't think about it that much. The one instance I can remember when race was an issue between us was when she and I were playing on the swingset—we were maybe eleven or twelve—and this white boy ran by. She said jokingly, "There's your boyfriend!" And I said real quick, "Un-uh! Not that white boy!" She didn't really take offense, but she did say she thought it was weird for me to have said it. When I thought about it later on, I realized that there was something inherently strange about my instant reflex to pass that boy off because he was white. It hadn't registered in my mind as I was saying it, and the only reason it registered at all was because my friend made mention of it. I also thought about how I would have felt if it had been the reverse and I called a black boy her boyfriend. If she had said, "No way! Not that black boy!" or "Not that nigger!" I'da been all over her.

I had lots of other white friends in both grade school and high school. The first girl who approached me on my first day of second grade was a white girl. That initial encounter made the next ten years of going to school with white kids a little easier. My friends from Shepherd Park started treating me different when I went to a private school in the fourth grade. They'd say things like, "Why you wanna be around all those rich, snobby, white kids?" and "I bet you can't even dance no more!" as if the white kids' lack of rhythm had rubbed off on me. Most of the time I felt that their comments came out of jealousy and I didn't really let it bother me. It was hurtful to be judged all of a sudden by the kids who I had played with for so long. But I felt like whoever didn't like my actions, I didn't need. I don't know where that mentality comes from. It's guarded, I know, but the majority of my values come from my gut. I don't mean to discredit my parents or to not make notice of the people in my life who have influenced and affected me, but I do know that I don't let people control my actions. And my actions are instinctive.

In the fourth grade, there were forty girls in my class. Six of us were black. Every Friday we went swimming. Now, when the white girls got out of the pool, they just blew dry their hair and were out, but the six of us black girls had to take an extra ten or fifteen minutes every time to do our hair; braiding, combing, pressing, or whatever. See, the constitution teaches us that everyone is equal, but if I have to take ten minutes longer than the white girls just to get home after swimming, then we are not equal. Blacks and whites are different and we are allowed separate, sometimes prolonged, privileges. We have to acknowledge that difference before we can even bring equality into the equation. I'm not trying to say that anyone is better than anyone else. When I was going through puberty and talking with other girls, trying to find out what girlhood was all about, I found out that white girls wash their hair every day, while us black girls wash our hair once a week. That may sound irrelevant to the larger picture, but if no one is teaching white girls about black history, they're going to logically think that we are just plain dirty folks. They are not going to know that because black hair is naturally coarse and dry, we have to grease our scalps, and washing our hair every day would make our hair break off. The point is, none of this means that we can't be different and equal at the same time; it means that we aren't.

My self-image problems have never been about my appearance or my gender. I never thought about my body shape much. I couldn't have cared less about my body, as a matter of fact, or any of that weird, gawky, breast-and-hip-developing stuff. My self-image problem was about making the grade. Going to private schools brought a lot of pressure with it. I've always been labeled as an underachiever. My teachers would always say that I was far more intelligent than my grades implied. In seventh grade, I was getting D's in history and math. At that point, I started thinking about suicide. I directly equated my scholastic achievements with who I was as a person. Everyone in my school was smart, but if you got average or below average grades, you were nothing, which was worse than being dumb. My school fostered this sort of competitive atmosphere, which was difficult to break free from or feel like an individual in.

I managed to stay on a steady and progressive track when I got to high school and began to feel more intact. Then I had this crush on a black boy at my school, but he didn't even know I existed. I only saw him with white girls. It was obvious and evident that most if not all of the black boys in my school wanted nothing to do with black girls, which was sort of traumatizing. You can't really come away from an experience like that without feeling like there is something wrong with you. In the final analysis, I ended up feeling that there was something wrong with him, but it was hell getting there.

In my senior year of high school, I was vice president of the student body, president of the black student union, and president of the school's singing group. I had all of these leadership skills, but I still felt slighted because I was the one doing all the leading and I felt entitled to some leading myself. Oh, I got angry sometimes. My teachers didn't mind that I was a leader, they minded that I was a leader with anger and attitude. They told me that I needed to find other ways to state my opinions. I didn't really feel obliged. By the end of the year, I had a 2.6 grade point average, and after a rough year at home, I felt alone. I tried applying to colleges as an independent. I applied to Brown, Stanford, and Dartmouth, which had written me a letter after having seen me speak on a panel for black youth on C-SPAN. But Dartmouth ended up turning me down, along with Brown and Stanford. Finally, my guidance counselor told me that I would have to find a school with a rolling admissions and a better-than-average financial aid program. Talladega College in Talladega, Alabama offered me a full scholarship and told me all I had to do was pay for my airfare. It hasn't turned out to be the right school for me, and I am planning on transferring to Loyola University in New Orleans. I've always considered myself to be a very open-minded person—I like different kinds of music, literature, and art—but I have found the students at Talladega to be very judgmental and close-minded in many ways. If I don't end up liking Loyola, at least I'll have the diversity of New Orleans. To say that Talladega as a town pales in comparison to New Orleans would be the understatement of the year. I chose to go to college because I want an education and a degree, but also because I want to grow and develop and have interesting experiences.

At this point in my life, I don't feel limited. I know there are limitations that come with being black and female, but I try to focus on overcoming the obstacles. Instead of looking at what I can't do or what society says I can't do, I try to look at what I can do and go from there. Being self-contained isn't so much something I was born with, but I know what I see when I see it. I've gone through my life paying attention and being willing to question and change situations if need be. There are many things that I know I will do with my life. I know that my poetry will be published one day. I look at poets like Ntozake Shange for the inspiration and courage to make writing a serious part of my life. I know that I will do something in communications and the media. I know that I will work with kids and encourage them to follow their dreams. And I know that I will be part of something big. Something revolutionary.

TIFFANY

Eleven
Birmingham, Alabama

What I'd like to say to black girls in America is that it's okay to be who they are and to express what they want to express. And what I'd like to say to white people in America is that I am not offended by their prejudices; if they want to presume that I am offended, then I'm going to presume that it is not my responsibility to educate them in any sort of detail.

My neighborhood is black. I've lived in white neighborhoods, too, and I've been the only black girl in a crowd of white kids. But I've never seen any reason to feel bad about it. There's nothing to feel bad about. In fact, I feel kind of special when I'm the only one. I feel like it's me against the world. I think it's silly to try and look for an experience that has made me feel different or has made me think that my struggle is harder than white people's struggle. You just gotta know who you are, and if you don't know, you can't look anywhere else but inside yourself.

For me, it is very important to have black friends. I have one good, close black friend at school. I also have white friends, but the fact is, if we are talking about something that might be considered "black," like a certain rap group or the language a rap group might use, my white friends are not going to understand, which is fine; they don't have to. Everyone is so upset that black people and white people don't all eat, sleep, and breathe the same everything, but if we did, we'd be in big trouble. I don't feel like I have to explain something like rap music to my white friends. If they want to listen to it, too, that's all right, but I don't know why they would think that I need to or can explain what it's like to listen to rap music or how I feel about it. And you know they'll ask, too. They'll say, "What is rap music all about?" What am I gonna tell them? Well, it has good beats.

I'm not defensive about the music I listen to and I don't really have a theory about it. But I have seen some videos on television that make me wonder about some of the music I listen to, like Snoop Doggy Dog. I think he's crazy offensive and I really don't understand why any woman would actually agree to be in his videos knowing that they're going to be exploited like they are. I don't want or need those women to be role models for me, but they do need to think about what they're doing to themselves and the message they are sending to young people. It's a shame, but if you are black in this society and you have the opportunity to be in front of millions of people, you need to pay attention to what you're doing and how you're doing it, especially if you are a female. It's bad enough that everything on the news talks about black females always being pregnant and on welfare. What's the difference between that and the black females actin' a fool in Snoop Doggy Dog's videos?

The school I'm at now is good. I went to a much bigger and more diverse school before starting at this one. It hasn't been the easiest transition, but I'm doing all right. I know it's a good opportunity for me. I like my classes and have some good teachers. I like science best, partly because I have a good teacher who takes the time to explain something if I don't understand and partly because I love that science is all about discovery. We do fun and exciting things in class, like go on scavenger hunts where we have to find and identify certain kinds of plants and stuff. I haven't decided what I want to be when I grow up. It's too early, I think, but I know I want to do something that involves discovering ideas and inventing things.

There are no black teachers at my school. The only black adults are the custodians. And that does have an impact on the students, I think. It would be nice to have even one black teacher at the school so that students, both black and white, could see that black people can be teachers, too and not just custodians. And also I think it would be important for the black students to be taught from the perspective of a black adult, not necessarily because there is a "black" way of teaching, but I know that it would be nice to feel like a teacher is talking to me and in some way understanding how I feel about certain things.

I'm not as concerned with black history as I am with black present. I think about black history sometimes, but I feel like it's more important to have the present be good for us. I don't have to think about black history to feel proud. I am proud *today*. I have a really solid family, which I feel lucky about. My mom is the kind of woman who cares a lot about people but doesn't ever go so far as to lose sight of herself. My dad and I are really close. He's a fireman. I haven't gone with him to any fires yet, but I think I will one day. I worry about him sometimes, but then I'll sit down and have a talk with him and feel better. We can talk about anything. He's always there for me. I think his most admirable quality is that he's weird. You know, he's not afraid to do anything at all—I mean anything. He is really fearless.

I have one older brother and he goes to a larger, more diverse school than the school I go to. I think being black means something different for boys than it does for girls. I think for boys everything rides on being tough and being cool. And being cool doesn't include hanging out with white people at all, as in the thought doesn't even fit into the picture. Somehow it seems like black girls can be more comfortable around white people. I don't know why, although I'm sure there's a reason. I just know that there are real serious pressures for black boys in society today and I try not to mess with it too much.

I have close white girlfriends at school. They're close, but not *real* close. There is a fine line between close and real close, but I guess what it really comes down to is trust. And see, it's the same with the way I feel about being black: I don't think about it; I just *know*. With my white friends, I don't think about being close or real close, I just know that there is a difference between being close and real close. For example, I take karate, and I am the only black girl in the class. See, I don't feel like an outcast because I'm pretty good at karate. But then again, one time I was at a karate tournament and I scored the highest on my team as well as against the other team. But the first-place trophy was given to another girl on my team who was white. I was mad, but it's almost like I know things like this are going to happen and it takes a lot of courage to keep getting up and moving on. When you just know things, there isn't a whole lot of time or really much use in trying to figure out why they are what they are.

I claim the right to be Tiffany and Tiffany is many things. I claim the right to play basketball, study science, do karate, listen to rap music, love my parents, be as loud as I please, and have an attitude that separates me from everyone else. My attitude can be all that or real chill, but whatever it is, it's mine. And if anyone has a problem with that, they can speak to me directly.

EPILOGUE

Last February I was asked to lead a workshop at a conference addressing the subject of girls in society and education. The conference was led by a well-known Harvard psychologist and social researcher whose keynote address was, in effect, an ardent proposal that the three hundred or so educators in attendance think of girls from all races and social classes when the term "girls" was used throughout the program. The fact that she had to so blatantly urge on this sense of awareness to three hundred educated adults was very disheartening, although not at all surprising. This prominent social researcher went on to discuss the ever present and, in my opinion, overindulgent issue of low self-esteem in young girls, attributing this pervasive lack of girl confidence to the matter of eating disorders.

I had been asked to lead a workshop on black girls in society and education, or more politically termed, "African-American Girls Coming of Age." This title seemed somewhat confusing after the keynote address, since the participants had been asked to think of girls from all racial, ethnic, and class backgrounds throughout the conference. Yet, my workshop was offered on the subject of black girls specifically, while the rest of the workshops were on the subject of "girls" in general.

Quite coincidentally, the night before the conference I had seen a story on the six o'clock news about eating disorders, and how continuously and disturbingly inoperable the issue is among young women and girls in America today. The focus region was a typical university campus; which means the typical university campus student body—which also means, before any other analysis or criticism, no black students. From firsthand experience, I can tell you that black students are an unknown and unwelcome entity on America's large, codified university campuses, and yet, high-school advisors still wonder why black students set their sights on black colleges.

The broadcast journalist reporting the story talked to several white freshman college girls about their body image and low self-esteem. At one point the reporter gathered four or five of these girls at one table and they proceeded to discuss the issue in a roundtable forum. The most common and repeated themes were about self-esteem, competition with other girls over who can lose the most weight, being an overachiever or a perfectionist, and reaching the ideal body so that they would be more attractive to boys. And the reporter nodded, appearing earnestly attentive while at the same time unabashedly leading the girls' answers with rhetorical questions. The wrap-up on the story said something about how these girls, at whatever cost, are caught in an obsessive trap of desire to attain the "perfect body." As the camera panned out to indicate the end of the story, the screen faded into an image of a young female model proudly parading her skeletal body down a runway.

One aspect of the news story that I found particularly interesting was that although the issue of eating disorders is repeatedly addressed with avid concern on a national level, the ideal body that young women with eating disorders aspire to have is still referred to by experts in the field as "perfect." This of course implies that everything else is imperfect, and while people might benevolently say that being imperfect is only human, you ask any young white girl in our society today if she would rather be humanly imperfect or inhumanly perfect and see what she says.

Anorexia and bulimia are both serious diseases; they are in fact violent social demands that can never ever be met by most young women in America. But it is an exclusive issue. It is a white issue. Those black girls and women in America who are plagued by either of these diseases have become resigned, whether knowingly or not, to their gradual descent into a white social behavior. What makes eating disorders a white issue is, first, the ideal model of beauty is white, and it is the ideal model of beauty that instigates and perpetuates eating disorders. Second, pondering the concept and living the reality of low self-esteem is a luxury of self-involvement that black girls cannot afford. For young white girls with eating disorders, human survival and sense of identity is not "at risk," so to speak. White girls have more options by way of their inherent and racially superior resources. In other words, young black girls have neither the time nor the opportunity to concern themselves with the contemplation of self-esteem.

Last winter at the private school where I teach, we had an assembly on eating disorders. As our guest speaker tried to goad the girls into admitting their deep-seated body denial, one of the black girls brought up the issue of cultural differences in terms of body image. The speaker smiled, said, "Good point," and then promptly dismissed the concept. It is instances like this when I feel compelled to speak on behalf of young black girls in America.

However, if it is not eating disorders, it is hair. Out of the fifty or so girls that I interviewed for this book, 90 percent of them had straightened and/or permed hair. Young black girls and older black women alike battle with hair in a similar way that young white girls and older white women battle with weight. And still, it is because of the white image of beauty that is constantly shoved in our faces by the media, which, like it or not, however questionable, delineates the American dream. Black girls and their mothers spend upward of sixty dollars every time they get their hair straightened (about every six weeks) and between one and three hundred dollars for braided extensions (about every two months), which are the two accepted and respected black hairstyles in America today. Both styles represent the hope of emulating long, flowy, touchable hair—white hair.

The process of straightening black hair is both time-consuming as well as tremendously unhealthy. What straightens naps is chemical lye, which gives you some idea of how tenacious black hair is. Extensions take a minimum of seven hours to braid in. Although, like eating disorders, the issue of black hair is engendered by the ideal of white beauty, the issue of black hair is more an issue of practicality than of vanity. This is to say, black hair is hard to negotiate, no two ways about it.

Our hair grows out rather than down, it is kinky as opposed to silky, it is thick as opposed to thin, it is ornery as opposed to obedient, it is sensual as opposed to sexy. And in a white, puritanical, and patriarchal society, all of these things don't quite add up. In the sixties when "black was beautiful," the afro was a time-honored exception to the rule. Since then, black girls and women have exorcised and crucified their natural hair both in an effort to control it as well as to suit the desires of their male counterparts, who are haplessly and often unknowingly loyal to America's image of beauty.

This of course is a mixed message to black girls: Black males want their females to have hips, tummies, thighs, and big butts, but they also want them to have straight hair. Any MTV or BET video can confirm this theory. Interestingly enough, the things that white girls and women hate about their bodies (the aforementioned hips, tummies, thighs, and butts) are the things that make them women in the most essential, integral way while hair is an effect. So black girls and women are able to sustain their essential womanliness but have slight difficulty bargaining their American aesthetic.

As educators of young girls, both black and white—and we are all educators to some extent—we have an obligation to differentiate between those issues that are racial and cultural and those that are societal. It is not useful for us to be ambiguous or diplomatic in these matters. What we need to understand is that black people and the children of black people have issues that are separate from and by no means equal to those of white people and the children of white people. This is a simple concept. The fight for equality is dead. Our greatest hope is to understand a few things, the least of which is our hair and body politics. But that's another book.

Black and white America have different codes of ethics. If black people look for other black people to be around, to talk and listen to, to dance with, to love and struggle with, we are not advocating segregation, nor are we black nationalists. We are loving the folks and shouting out to one another because we need to. A big shout out from me and the *Sugar* girls!

—Rebecca Carroll
February 26, 1996
Cambridge, Massachusetts